THE SCHOOL SYSTEM OF NORWAY

This edition published by Lector House in 2024

ISBN: 978-93-6138-951-1

Lector House LLP
Registered Office: H. No. 96, Block C, Tomar Colony,
Burari, Delhi – 110084, India
info@lectorhouse.com
www.lectorhouse.com

THE SCHOOL SYSTEM OF NORWAY

DAVID ALLEN ANDERSON

2024

LECTOR HOUSE LLP

THE SCHOOL SYSTEM OF NORWAY

BY

DAVID ALLEN ANDERSON, PH.D.

AUTHOR'S PREFACE

This account is a descriptive statement of the organization, management, operation, and efficiency of the public school system of Norway. The intent has been to consider only the more vital features, those essentials which definitely shape the products of educational endeavor. Many topics of interest have been touched but briefly while others have been omitted altogether. Some attention has been given to pointing out good qualities of the Norwegian schools and to indicating wherein we might improve our own.

The materials entering into the make-up of this dissertation were gathered during a summer and autumn devoted to travel and study in Norway. Much time was spent in study at the University Library in Christiania and still more in the visitation of schools. It was with pleasure that I availed myself of the opportunity to see the schools in operation. I observed recitations throughout the entire program of study in every grade from the kindergarten to the University. I also visited many special schools and other educational institutions both public and private. Further than this, I was benefited by frequent conferences with the leading educators of the country and by almost constant associations with schoolmen, patrons, and students. These personal investigations enabled me to become familiar with the spirit and work of the schools, and they furnish background for a large part of the content of this treatise. Since no adequate account of the schools of Norway is in print, the authority for this work has been gained chiefly from school laws, annual reports from the Department of Ecclesiastical and Educational Affairs (chiefly statistical), and the individual research referred to above.

It was my good fortune to be provided with official credentials as holder of a Traveling Fellowship for study in Norway from the State University of Iowa; a commission to study the school system of Norway from His Excellency, B. F. Carroll, the Governor of the State of Iowa; and a letter of introduction to Norway's educational executives from Hon. Elmer Ellsworth Brown, at that time Commissioner of Education for the United States. These credentials had the effect of intensifying the already superior courtesy and obliging disposition of the Norwegian officials and schoolmen, who gave me free access to every facility for the pursuance of my work within the state and voluntarily offered their cooperation whenever I might desire it. Their gracious exemplification of the spirit of brotherly kindness made my work among them a constant delight. I desire to express my gratitude to the Norwegians wherever I traveled for the rare cordiality characterizing my reception among them and to acknowledge my obligations to J. K. Qvigstad, *chef for Kirk-og Undervisningsdepartmentet;* Knut Johannes Hougen, *byraachef for Undervisningsvaesen;* A. H. Raeder, *Undervisningsraadets* formand; Johan Andreas

Johnsen, *Skoledirektoren i Kristiania stift*; Otto Andreas Anderssen, *Bestyrer og forstelaerer i det Paedagogiske Seminar for Laerere red hoiere Almenskoler*, for valuable suggestions and careful reading and criticism of the entire work in manuscript; further to Iowa's Board of Education and the Graduate Faculty of the State University of Iowa for the appointment which made possible the investigation; to Professor F. E. Bolton, who first suggested that I make the study and who has constantly been to me a wise counsellor and a willing co-operator; and finally to my wife who, through all, has been both critic and companion.

DAVID ALLEN ANDERSON.

The State University of Iowa,
Iowa City,
May, 1912.

REVIEWER'S PREFACE

Kristiania den 16 februar 1912.

Jeg har med stor fornoielse gjennemlaest Mr. David A. Andersons fremstilling av Norges Undervisningsvaesen og fundet den i all vaesentlige ting korrekt, fuldstaendig og oplysende. Gjennem personlig iagttagelse, samtale med kompetente maend og studium av den vigtigste litteratur er det lykkes forfatteren at danne sig en klar og noiagtig forestilling om de norske skolers ordning og saeregne arbeidsformer i deres historiske tilblivelse og nuvaerende vilkaar. Hans reflektioner og domme vedner om paedagogiske indsight og uavhaengig opfatning. Det er mulig at han nu og da er noget tilboielig til at domme vel gunstig om vore skoleinstitutioners effektivitet og vort folks interesse og offervillighed for at gjorc denne saa stor some mulig, men dette for haenge sammen med at han ser tingene mot en bakgrund av amerikanske forhold, som han onsker reformeret.

Jeg har ikke havt anledning til at kontrollere i det enkelte de statistiske opgaver forfatteren meddeler, men da disse er hentet ut fra officielle kilder tviler jeg ikke paa at de er rigtige.

Professor dr Otto Anderssen,
Principal of the Pedagogical Seminary annexed to the University of Christiania.

(Translation)

Christiania, February 16, 1912.

I have, with great pleasure, read through Mr. David A. Anderson's presentation of Norway's school system and found it in all essentials correct, complete and illuminating. Through personal observation, conversation with competent men and study of the most important literature, the author has succeeded in getting a clear and exact view of the Norwegian school methods and characteristic forms of work in their historical development and present condition. His reflections and judgments testify to pedagogical insight and independence of views. It may be that now and then he is somewhat inclined to judge too favorably as to the efficiency of our institutions and the interest of our people and their readiness to sacrifice in order to make this efficiency as high as possible, but this may be due to the fact that he views it against a background of American conditions, which he desires to improve.

I have not taken occasion to verify in detail the statistical tables the author includes, but since they have been gathered from official sources I do not doubt that they are correct.

Professor Dr. Otto Anderssen,
Principal of the Pedagogical Seminary, affiliated with the University of Christiania.

EDITOR'S PREFACE

The most pressing problems of education at the present time are those of organization and administration of educational forces. Problems of method of instruction though important are entirely subsidiary, for if all the people can be aroused to a desire for education and then be shown ways and means of attaining it the very desire for education will be the most important factor in learning.

No means of studying questions of organization and administration are so valuable as the comparative. Various studies of education in foreign countries have been made, but there still exists a need for many more investigations. Norway has furnished a great many illustrious statesmen, scientists and literary masters, and is also a country abounding in men of a high type of valor, physical prowess, honesty and industry, and consequently the educational ideals and practices which prevail there should be worthy of most careful consideration. Heretofore, only fragmentary accounts of Norway's educational system have been available in the English language. At the writer's suggestion, Mr. Anderson made a trip abroad for the purpose of studying the system at first hand. His intimate acquaintance with the language was a prime essential in acquiring an understanding through observation and reading. That he has made an accurate interpretation is attested by the foreword of one of Norway's eminent scholars and that he has made an interesting account will be conceded by all who peruse the pages. It is hoped that many more studies of a similar nature will follow in the near future.

FREDERICK E. BOLTON,
State University of Washington,
Seattle, April 8, 1913.

CONTENTS

CHAPTER II
TEACHERS

CHAPTER III
COURSES OF STUDY IN STATE SCHOOLS

CHAPTER IV
INTERPRETATIVE CONCLUSIONS

CHAPTER I

BACKGROUND AND ORGANIZATION

I. INTRODUCTION

1. History of Norway (brief sketch)

The history of mankind in Norway covers a period of at least five thousand years and includes a great variety of interesting incidents and conditions. The accounts of the earlier ages may be read only in archaeological formations, while for more recent times, these silent records are supplemented and enriched by traditions. All such accounts are of deep interest and significance but only in a measure reliable. We have no really authentic information regarding Norway's political history until the reign of Harald the Fair Haired (860-930). We do know, however, that, previous to his establishment of the sovereign state of Norway in 872, the people had known only the rule of numerous petty, warring earls and kings. Besides this, the entire country had been subjected to the devastations of the vikings. These sea robbers were the terror of all the coast countries in western Europe and the British Isles until about the year 900 when sea robbery at home was abolished, and the Norsemen became colonizers, migrating to surrounding islands, the west and south of Europe, and probably America. Now when piracy began to decline the people rose to a higher plane of living, and the prosperity attained through peace and industry was found to be the more desirable. A long succession of kings, some good and some evil, ruled the land. Paganism was gradually overcome, and about the year 1,000 Christianity was established.

From this time on, for several centuries, the country experienced only moderate visible progress though large gains were made in potential powers. In 1381, Norway entered into a union with Denmark and remained in large measure subject to her power until 1814. This period of more than four hundred years was a season of little good and of great hardships to the people. Their development received little attention, the resources of the country and the cause of education were neglected, and the masses were not recognized in a way that would tend to their enlightenment and progress. The entire nation suffered from international difficulties as well as from oppression at home. Conditions remained unimproved and the latent powers of the people, which had been accumulating for generations, found no adequate means for expression.

When in 1814 the treaty of Kiel, sanctioned by the European powers, forced Norway into an unwilling union with Sweden, the Norwegians revolted; and, in their attempt to liberate themselves, adopted a constitution for their government.[1] Their revolt created ill feelings on the part of the Swedes while the demands for complete sovereignty by Sweden were resented by the Norwegians. The adoption of this constitution by the people of Norway and their standing so tenaciously for its recognition are manifestations of the spirit which had been developing among them for centuries. They believed that they were being imposed upon and stood firm for their rights. They had felt the crushing hand of foreign rule, they had observed the benefits of independence, they had developed confidence in their own powers, and now they were converted to the idea that the time for home rule was upon them. Civil liberty was their dream. State rights came to be demanded. Their time to act in a decisive manner had come. The people had grown into a nation deserving and in need of larger powers, and their best advancement was in great measure dependent upon the exercise of these powers. Conditions then justified their demands and Sweden, appreciating the situation, yielded, acknowledged the independence of Norway, and agreed to govern in accordance with the newly adopted constitution. On the other hand, Norway acceded to the demands of Sweden in accepting the King of Sweden as theirs also.

Now for nearly one hundred years this union was maintained. Comparative peace and prosperity prevailed and the outlook seemed favorable for both nations. Sweden profited because of the new relations, and Norway gained in strength and power through her experience in individual initiative and governmental duties generally. While the relations between the two countries were in the main friendly, on various occasions Norway felt that her rights were not always respected. The people craved larger privileges, more recognition among the nations of the world, and the exercise of greater authority. The functioning of capacities that had long lain dormant revealed to her the powers that were still latent. Norway became eager for absolute independence and these feelings rose to larger and larger proportions until desires became demands. All the people were ready and offered their services, their fortunes (whether large or scant), and their lives in the cause of freedom. Finally, formally, and without bloodshed, the bonds uniting the two countries were severed in 1905 and Norway became an independent nation.

2. Geographical features

Having briefly sketched the history of the country let us now turn our attention to its geography. Norway, as we all know, lies in the northwestern part of Europe, and measures over one thousand one hundred miles from north to south and from two hundred to nearly five hundred miles from east to west. Politically it is divided into eighteen counties (*Amter*) and the cities of Christiania and Bergen. These counties are subdivided into six hundred sixty-six townships or communes (*Kommuner*) which are again divided into school districts or circles (*Kredser*) numbering in all five thousand nine hundred seventy.[2]

The area is approximately one hundred and twenty-five thousand square miles. Nearly all of it is made up of mountains which have no regularity in distri-

[1] The Constitution (*Grundlov*) adopted at Eidsvold, Norway, May 17, 1814.

[2] Statistics for 1907—the last published.

bution, a large portion of them being merely heaps of barren rock thrown up in conglomerate masses. The valleys are as numerous and irregular as the mountains. In them are lakes, rivers, and waterfalls, their waters pure and clear as crystal. The lakes differ greatly in outline and size. The rivers in their windings dash furiously through precipitous, rugged, rocky channels, or glide murmuringly through quiet valleys until they reach the fjords which appear like huge arms of the sea, reaching deep into the earth and extending far inland. The waterfalls vary from mere threads tinkling into tiny pools to great torrents gushing over dizzy precipices. Viewed in combination these features present an infinite variety of exquisitely beautiful scenes.

The climate of Norway is greatly diversified owing to the wide range in latitude and the influence of the Gulf stream. In the northern part and on the highest mountains there are vast fields of snow during the entire year, while in some of the sheltered portions along the western coast, the climate is well adapted to the cultivation of some of the tropical plants. It is, of course, essential that all plants that are cultivated be of rapid growth and of quick maturity, since their seasons are quite short. The atmospheric conditions are excelled nowhere. Few locations on the earth enjoy such freshness or provide so much mental and physical invigoration. Just the joy of living is more than recompense for all one's expense and trouble in going for a season into this summer home or nature.

Being situated so far to the north the days of summer are very long while those of winter are extremely short. This is noticeable even in the southern part of the country, and as one goes farther north it is more and more striking until upon reaching the arctic circle the summer traveler has the unique experience of seeing the sun at midnight. It is visible for weeks or months at a time, according to whether one is near the circle or farther toward the pole. For corresponding periods during the winter seasons the sun does not appear at all. It should not be inferred that these sunless days are intensely dark and gloomy. On the contrary, they, as well as the midnight sun, have fascinations peculiar to themselves and are of deep interest, especially to the novice in that latitude. The glitter of the stars, the glow of the moon, and the palpitating brilliance of the northern lights, combine with the light reflected from the vast snow fields and compensate in part for the absence of the direct rays from the sun.

The industries and occupations of the Norwegians are dependent in large measure upon environing conditions. Nearly one-fourth of the country is covered with a heavy growth of timber; hence, lumbering affords a large part of the most profitable employment. Much of the mountainous land can be used only for pasturage and, as a result, dairying claims considerable attention. Only a very small portion of the area (about four per cent) is suitable for agriculture and owing to this limitation of opportunity, comparatively few of the people are farmers. Their numerous fisheries supply cargoes, and train loads of fresh and cured fish to the markets of the world. Fishing is, in fact, one of the most important industries, and a large percentage of the wage earners of the country engage in it. Since the bulk of their travel and transportation is by water, a great many become sailors. A certain amount of manufacturing also is done, and this provides another means of earning a livelihood. The fact that nearly all of the people are gathered into cities, towns, and settlements along the coast, is explained by a consideration of the activities and conditions herein set forth.

3. National characteristics, aims and ideals

The people of Norway are large of stature, vigorous, and alert in mind and body. They have ever been undaunted in their efforts to overcome the great, natural barriers to progress and to secure what they believed would be for their well-being. Toiling patiently and persistently, suffering hardships on land and perils at sea, they have developed the well-known characteristics of their sturdy race. The long, rigorous winters taught the people to provide amply for the needs of the future, and they learned also the economy of making every endeavor count for permanency. It has been and is still their aim and intent to so direct their efforts that their citizens may experience and enjoy not only in the present the best conditions made possible by the world's highest attainments, but that later generations also may reap valuable benefits therefrom. They realize that it is easily possible for today's provisions to supply the best for the present, and at the same time to bless tomorrow and the next day and all the coming years.

The Norwegians are as democratic in mind and disposition as any people of the earth. They demand that the masses shall receive whatever benefit may come from prosperity at home, from their relations with other nations, or from legislation. They advocate further that right now is the time to increase opportunities, to multiply privileges, to raise standards of living, and to insure through conservative action a substantial basis on which the coming generations may safely build. In accord with their aims and ideals they study the questions of education, labor and capital, and many others of vital interest to the people. They seek out sources, eliminating the undesirable and cultivating those of favorable growth and fruitage. Recognizing their own resourcefulness and ability, the Norsemen strive to gain for themselves and for their descendants material prosperity and true culture. To these ends they foster educational advantages for all, the development of the arts and sciences, and the elevation of labor.

Educationally, they have ever been desirous of providing the best possible advantages. During the latter part of the nineteenth century and the few years of the present one, they have been in a position to put into execution a number of advance ideas which they have done without hesitation. Being observant of what other nations provide they have been ready to select from various sources whatever good they found, to eliminate any undesirable features which revealed themselves, and to strengthen the weaker points. Though they have been forced by conditions to assume and maintain a conservative attitude toward every new project or attempt at reform, they have been also too democratic to permit tradition or precedent to bind them down or to hinder them in making changes in their school system, which they were convinced by experience or study would be for their good. In harmony with this they have been eager to make revisions where necessary; to introduce new features, which had been tested at home or abroad and found successful; and to cast aside relics of the past, unnecessary phases of work, and those things which might be supplanted by materials of superior advantage or value to the people served. They have become habituated to examining the new from every conceivable viewpoint, to finding its foundations, to testing its values, and to weighing its effects. When a thing has been thoroughly studied it is accepted or rejected according to whether it is adjudged desirable or undesirable for their use under existing conditions. In their effort to answer the demands of the people and to supply their needs, schools have been established according to local requirements. That is to say, every community enjoys school advantages, and every child in the entire state is privileged to receive instruction for a certain number of weeks each year at the expense of the state. All children are required to attend the schools of the state at least twelve weeks each year for seven years, or to receive instruction elsewhere which is equivalent to the amount required. In the more populous places higher schools also are provided for those who desire to take advantage of the opportunities afforded in them.

II. DIFFERENTIATION OF SCHOOLS

1. Primary School—Rural and City

It was early recognized by the Norwegians that through the means of education, better than any other way, they could develop a people qualified to pursue the arts, to cultivate the sciences, to appreciate and enjoy the highest culture, and to maintain and develop their noblest ideals of citizenship and richest conceptions of statehood. Having these objects in mind they endeavored to establish schools of instruction and training along every legitimate line. Beginning with the most essential they worked unceasingly, providing additional worthy kinds of instruction as rapidly as possible, until their efforts resulted in their present school system.

Perhaps the most important feature of their work was the establishment of primary schools, which furnish general education. These schools provide seven years of elementary instruction for children between the ages of seven and fourteen years, and are literally the people's schools (*Folkeskoler*). The law requires that pupils must be regular in attendance, and that parents, who fail to have their children in school in harmony with the provisions of the law, be fined according to the seriousness and extent of the offense. It is further provided that these schools shall be in operation for at least twelve weeks in the year, and that this time may be extended according to local demands or needs. As a matter of fact, nearly all of them in the cities and many of them in the country operate forty weeks per year. As a consequence of liberal provisions and enforced regulations, Norway has achieved an eminent place educationally among the nations of the world.

In the rural sections primary schools are held in comfortable, well equipped, and conveniently located schoolhouses and are taught by competent teachers who live near by in homes provided for them. In a few remote, rugged sections of the country, where children are few and scattering or where locations accessible to all cannot be found, they have no fixed schools, but instead what are termed ambulatory schools (*Omgangskoler*). There are no schoolhouses in these districts but the officials designate certain houses[3] as the places where children go at stated times to receive instruction. The teacher meets the children of the neighborhood in a given home and teaches them for a specified time, passes to the next designated place, and continues until his rounds are completed. Formerly, a very large number of these schools existed, but as roadways were extended or improved and the people became able to erect and maintain schoolhouses, the demand for ambulatory schools decreased until now nearly all of them are supplanted by fixed schools. In 1837, ninety-two per cent of the children attending school in the country were taught in ambulatory schools, while in 1907 this was the case with less than one per cent of them.

2. Secondary

In all the cities and towns excellent educational advantages are provided. Usually their school year consists of forty weeks of six days each. Every provision is made for the welfare of the children; excellent instructors are secured, and the equipment for teaching purposes is of the best procurable. Furthermore, no pains are spared in guarding the children from physical discomfort and immoral conditions or associations.

Simultaneously with the development of the elementary schools secondary education moved along advance lines. In 1814, when Norway became an independent state there were but four of the higher classical (*laerde*) schools within her borders. These were the historic cathedral schools (*Kathedralskoler*) which had been established for centuries. As time passed, other secondary schools were organized. Higher education was reorganized in 1869 and again in 1896, when by act of the Storthing secondary education was made to include the middle school and the gymnasium. The enactment defines these schools and states their aim as follows: "The middle school is a school for children, which, in union with the primary school, gives its pupils a complete, thorough, general education, adapted to the receptivity of childhood. The gymnasium is a school for young people, which on the foundation of the middle school, leads on to a complete, higher, general education, which may also serve as a basis for scientific studies. Both middle school and gymnasium shall contribute to the religions and moral training of the pupils, and it should also be their common aim to develop the pupils both mentally and physically into competent young people."[4] The act requires that the middle school shall be no longer than four years, and that the gymnasial courses shall be of three years' duration.

The gymnasia of Norway take up the work where the middle schools leave off, and provide three years of instruction which concludes with the *examen artium*. The passing of this examination entitles the individual to become a student in the university. Previous to the time of entering the gymnasium the subjects of instruction are uniform for all; here they branch into two or three lines, any one of which may be selected by the pupil and followed to its completion. The main

[3] The law requires the opening of residences having sufficient room for the accommodation of these groups of pupils for instructional purposes. Law for Rural Schools, Sec. 41.

[4] Law for Higher State Schools, Sec. 2.

divisions of the work are represented in the names of the courses—the *Real* and the Linguistic-Historical. The latter of these is again divided in some schools, one of its two lines including Latin. The *Real* course of instruction is largely scientific while the Linguistic-Historical, true to its name, embodies a large amount of language and history. In case the course including Latin is offered, Latin replaces some of the work in modern languages and history.

The middle school, then, is the second step in the educational ladder and builds upon the work previously done in the primary school. No middle school is privileged to include work lower down than the sixth grade. In other words, the primary schools are the only ones which are authorized to present the work of the first five grades or years of school instruction. The courses of study are so arranged that a child may pass from the primary school after completing the fifth grade and enter directly upon the studies in the regular four year course of the middle school. On the other hand a pupil may continue in the primary school until its completion—seven years—and then enter a middle school and finish its requirements in three years. While nearly all middle schools present a four year course there are a few which offer only three years of instruction. In order to enter these latter schools the child must have finished the seven years of instruction in the primary schools. Middle schools are under the inspection of state officials and a uniform standard of work is required of all of them. The middle school examination which marks the completion of the middle school course is exactly the same for all pupils in the state. In any given year all who take the examinations write on exactly the same questions on a specified hour of a certain day.

3. The University and other schools

The Royal Frederik University, established by King Frederik in 1811, furnishes the summit of educational endeavor. Its five faculties—(1) theology, (2) law, (3) medicine, (4) mathematics and science, and (5) history and philosophy—represent the best products of the country and maintain standards of efficiency paralleling the achievements of the day. Besides the five faculties already mentioned there are (1) The Practical Theological Seminary for the training of ministers and (2) The Pedagogical Seminary (affiliated) for special training of teachers. Through the endeavors of the faculties and seminaries enumerated, the necessary professions, scientific organizations, and philosophic societies are supplied with men of eminent qualifications. The state also is supplied from the same source with individuals capable of attending to the affairs of state in a dignified and competent manner.

To aid prospective teachers and to maintain high professional standards, Norway early established a Teachers' Seminary in each of its six dioceses (*Stifter*). Having made this ample provision for the training of teachers, they were in a position to require a certain amount of professional preparation of all candidates for appointment to teaching positions. Adherence to this laudable principle has saved the state from an overflow of incompetent instructors. While requirements were very low for a long time, the increasing supply of qualified candidates for positions warranted successive shiftings of them to higher and higher standards. At present, the teachers of Norway, as a body, rank among the best in educational equipment, professional training, and morality.

Technical, agricultural, military, and naval schools have been established in order to keep pace with the world's developments along these lines. The technical school in Trondhjem opened in 1910, sets the requirements for admission as high as those at the university. Its work promises to be of unquestioned quality and its prospects are very bright. The students at this school come chiefly from the scientific course offered in the gymnasia or from the several preparatory technical schools of Norway. There are many of these lower technical schools doing excellent work and some of them are modeled after American schools. The work of the agricultural college and of the military and naval schools is more or less technical along their respective lines and meets certain requirements not elsewhere provided for. When one notes the variety of schools maintained by the Norwegian state, it is evident that it is the intent to provide for its citizens a very wide range of educational advantages, and at the same time to develop the capacities of young people until they are able to perform the offices of state and nation.

III. DISTRIBUTION OF SCHOOLS AND PUPILS

1. Primary—rural and city

The laws of Norway are specific in their requirements regarding education, and the people are at hand to provide the essential means for carrying out the demands. It is required that in each city or district in the entire realm there shall be the necessary number of schools to provide instruction for all children of school age. This is in answer to the law which makes a requirement of a certain minimum amount of education of all such children.

The primary schools are distributed in the cities, villages, and rural communes to suit the convenience of pupils attending. Other and higher schools are provided where most needed. As is true everywhere the bulk of work is done in the primary schools. Rural and city schools have their own laws and government, and are admirably adapted to the needs of their respective constituencies. As would be expected, the rural schools and the pupils attending them far outnumber those in the cities and towns. There are in the country five thousand, nine hundred and seventy schools attended by two hundred seventy-five thousand, one hundred and fifty-five pupils, while there are but sixty-one city school systems having an enrollment of ninety thousand, one hundred and twenty-nine pupils.[5] It is seen that there are about three times as many pupils in the rural primary schools as are found in the city primary schools. The distribution and care of the city school pupils are, however, much larger tasks than providing for those in the rural sections. In order to show conditions in a given city we insert Table I which indicates the number of classes and pupils in the several grades in the nineteen primary schools of Christiania, and also gives the totals for the entire city. Boys and girls attend the same school, but in this particular city they are generally separated into different rooms where they are taught by themselves. The schools are co-educational but not generally coinstructional. As the table will show, some of them are coinstruc-

[5] Statistics for 1907.

tional through a part of the course while only one follows this plan throughout its work.

In addition to the special features in this table, to which we have already called attention, it may be observed that the total number of boys', girls', and co-educational classes; the total number of boys and of girls in attendance at each school; and the average number of pupils per class in each school are also included.

The law limits the number of pupils in a class to thirty-five, except temporarily or in case of stringency in financial conditions, and in no case must there be more than forty.[6] It is seen in the table that the average is above thirty-five in all but one school, but it has been exceedingly difficult in the rapidly growing city of Christiania to avoid congestion in the schools. In only one of the nineteen schools does the general average come within the rule. If they plead economic stringency then the averages of all fall within the limits.

2. Secondary—middle school and gymnasium

Now a large percentage of children continue their education after the completion of the elementary course. In 1907, there were nine thousand, eight hundred and ninety-five pupils in the accredited middle schools,[7] and one thousand, five hundred and ninety-three in the gymnasia. About eighteen thousand others attended non-accredited secondary schools and those of still lower standards—evening schools, continuation schools, and various preparatory schools. Approximately two thousand were in technical schools and about one thousand in teachers' seminaries. Nearly every town of any considerable consequence has a middle school where pupils from the town and surrounding territory may receive its benefits. The larger cities have, in addition to a liberal supply of middle schools, one or more gymnasia, according to their size. The gymnasia draw from a wider territory than do the middle schools because they are fewer and farther apart.

3. Teachers' Seminaries

In addition to the six teachers' seminaries maintained by the state, there are four private ones—ten in all. Table II indicates the aggregate attendance at these institutions and the number of those who passed the advanced examinations during the years designated.

4. The University

The university, of course, draws its students from all over the State. It has an attendance of one thousand, three hundred or more, about five hundred and fifty of whom are annually enrolled direct from the gymnasia. These students represent the best products of the country and generally they work with earnestness and zeal.

[6] Law for City Schools, Sec. 5, as amended on August 15, 1908.

[7] Schools undertaking educational work of this character must meet specified standards in course of study, equipment, teaching staff, etc., to have their work accredited by the state.

TABLE I

Pupils in the Primary Schools of Christiania in the month of April, 1908

NUMBER OF CLASSES AND PUPILS IN THEM

Schools		1st Grade		2nd		3rd		4th		5th		6th		7th	
		Cl.	Pu.	Cl.	Pu.	Cl.	Pu.	Cl.	Pu.	Cl.	Pu.	Cl.	Pu.	Cl.	Pu.
A.	Boys	3	112	3	99	3	114	4	136	3	115	3	96	3	95
	Girls	3	107	3	113	3	116	3	105	3	111	3	101	2	83
B.	Boys	5	183	5	194	4	157	4	160	5	199	5	177	4	144
	Girls	5	178	5	184	5	196	4	149	5	188	4	151	4	149
C.	Boys	2	89	2	90	2	100	2	98	2	98	2	79	2	64
	Girls	2+1	99	2+1	96	2+1	101	2+1	95	2+1	97	2+1	89	2	77
D.	Boys	3	139	3	123	4	140	3	127	3	108	3	103	3	93
	Girls	3+1	119	3+1	132	3	117	3+1	139	3	028	3	110	3	101
E.	Boys	3	121	4	149	3	113	2	77	2	74	2	72	2	65
	Girls	3	115	4	152	3	101	3	116	3	115	2	77	2	60
F.	Boys	3	138	2	93	2	83	2	67	3	98	3	107	1	37
	Girls	3+1	122	2+1	102	2+1	104	3	104	2	77	2	79	2	65

G.	Boys	4	151	3	140	2	119	4	138	3	121	3	99	3	105
	Girls	4	147	4+1	157	4+1	148	4	134	3	106	2	80	3	93
H.	Boys	4	142	4	136	3	119	3	115	4	139	3	109	2	66
	Girls	3	131	3	136	4	131	4	142	3	102	2	80	2	69
I.	Boys	3	96	3	96	3	86	2	73	2	77	2	68	3	102
	Girls	2	79	2	68	2	82	2	79	2	68	2	71	3	102
J.	Boys	2	95	2	91	2	90	2	80	2	81	2	70	2	641
	Girls	2+1	87	2+1	109	2+1	98	3	93	2	66	2	68	2	661
K.	Boys	4	153	4	145	4	143	3	118	3	120	3	121	3	84
	Girls	5	170	4+1	153	4	139	4	154	3	123	3	103	3	93
L.	Boys	4	143	4	145	4	134	4	144	4	129	4	132	2	75
	Girls	4	158	4	148	4	141	4	132	4	136	4	157	4	131
M.	Boys	7	133	6	111	5	91	2	99	2	102	2	70	2	74
	Girls		136		108		115	2+2	124	2+2	115	3	97	2	72
N.	Boys	4	151	1	106	1	108	2	113	2	85	2	105	2	72
	Girls	3	109	1+4	125	1+3	127	2+2	108	2+1	100	2+2	106	2	64
O.	Boys		111		98		128		118		102		95		57
	Girls	5	90	5	98	7	126	6	104	5	88	5	98	4	73

		Cl.	Pu.	Cl.	Pu.	Cl.	Pu.	Cl.	Pu.	Cl.	Pu.	Cl.	Pu.	Cl.	Pu.	Cl.	Pu.
P.	Boys	3	126	2	83	3	116	3	103	3	103	2	68	3	96		
	Girls	3	113	3	117	3	105	3	113	3	99	2	80	3	100		
Q.	Boys	4	155	5	192	5	168	4	158	4	155	4	149	3	116		
	Girls	4	154	5+1	189	4	163	5	171	4	144	3	118	3	111		
R.	Boys		154		159		131		112	3	107	2	83	3	104		
	Girls		186		128		141		115	3	110	3+1	131	2	77		
S.	Boys	5	185	4	151	4	139	4	135	3	111	2	75				
	Girls	4	159	5	172	4	146	3	108	4	148	2	79				
Total	(Classes)		134		131		126		122		115		104		91		2
	(Pupils)		5036		4878		4676		4458		4235		3753		3099		43
Average number of pupils per class			37.6		37.3		37.1		36.5		36.8		36.1		34.1		
Schools for Abnormals																	
	Boys	4+1	47	7	54	5+1	57		46		66	6+1	65		30	2	19
	Girls		18		53		41		37		47		33		18		9

Cl.—Class.

Pu.—Pupils.

1.—Classes made up of children requiring individual attention.

	Total Classes			Total Pupils		Condensed table of all groups		
Schools	Boys'	Girls'	Coeds.	Boys	Girls	Classes	Pupils	Average for class.
A.	22	20		767	736	42	1503	35.8
B.	32	32		1214	1195	64	2409	37.6
C.	14	14	6	618	644	34	1262	37.1
D.	22	21	3	833	846	46	1679	36.5
E.	18	20		671	736	38	1407	37.0
F.	16	16	3	623	653	35	1276	36.5
G.	22	24	2	873	865	48	1738	36.2
H.	23	21		826	781	44	1607	36.5
I.	18	15		598	549	33	1147	34.8
J.	15	16	3	595	606	34	1201	35.3
K.	24	26		884	935	50	1819	36.4
L.	26	28		902	1003	54	1905	35.3
M.	8	9	22	680	767	39	1447	37.1
N.	14	13	13	740	739	40	1479	37.0
O.			37	709	677	37	1386	37.5
P.	19	20		695	727	39	1422	36.5
Q.	29	28		1093	1050	57	2143	37.6
R.	8	8	31	850	888	47	1738	37.0
S.	22	22		796	812	44	1608	36.5
Total number of Pupils	352	353	120	14967	15209	825	30176	36.6
Schools for Abnormals	3		39	384	256	42	640	15.6

TABLE II

Table Giving Attendance at Teachers' Seminaries and the Number Passing Advanced Examinations.

Year.	Attendance.	Took Examination. Male.	Female.	Total.
1901-02	755	204	135	339
1902-03	980	192	129	321
1903-04	953	216	184	400
1904-05	902	174	119	293
1905-06	955	208	147	355
	Totals	994	714	1,708
	Annual Average	199	143	342

Private schools have played an important role in Norway. They have had a long and interesting history. A number of them do part or all of the work represented by the state primary and secondary schools and teachers' seminaries. Most of them are located in the larger cities and receive recognition and patronage from some of the best homes in the land. Their influence upon education generally has been wholesome. The valuable and attractive features introduced by them have operated like spurs on those under state direction. The cooperative activity which has characterized the relationship between the two kinds of schools has resulted in the betterment of both and in the rapid advancement of educational ideals and activities throughout the state.

5. Private schools

There are, of course, some fundamental differences existing between them. The private schools charge a regular tuition in every grade of primary and secondary work. The state primary schools are free and the tuition in its secondary schools is less than that charged in the private schools. It is self-evident that private schools are dependent upon tuition receipts for both running expenses and profits, while the state and communal schools are supported largely by public taxation.[8] Paralleling so nearly the work of the state schools, yet being more expensive, the private schools have been under the necessity of offering certain inducements in order to secure pupils. They have been made attractive in location, in buildings, in equipment, in the personnel of their faculties, and in other ways, and their efforts have been richly rewarded as a rule.

All classes of schools are subject to state regulations and inspection. Certain

[8] The only difference between state and communal schools consists in the fact that in the one case the state and in the other a commune takes the initial step in the establishment of the school and bears the larger portion of the burden in its maintenance. The work of the two is uniform in every particular. They are together referred to as state schools in contrast to private schools.

definite requirements must be met before a private school may even begin to operate, and still higher standards must be maintained in order for the work to be accredited by the state. Standards of excellence are naturally set by state schools and the requirements fixed by the state inhibit the starting of inferior schools under the pretense of offering something "just as good." During recent years some of the private schools—those well-known and respected because of the nature of work and high standards of excellence maintained—have been given special recognition by the state, and a few of them receive annuities. When advancement in nature or improvement in quality of school work is rewarded by increase in patronage from the state, zest is furnished in the contest for first recognition.

Though the history of the rise, development and influence of the private schools of Norway, together with a discussion of their present status and worth, might furnish an interesting chapter, it becomes necessary to let this slight mention suffice and to confine this work to a treatise of the schools instituted and directed by the state. It may be added, however, that the work of the accredited private schools equals in quality and receives the same recognition as that done in state schools. For example, all graduates from the private gymnasia pass the same examinations for *artium* as those who complete the work of the state gymnasia and enter the university on exactly the same footing.

IV. PUPILS

1. Age in primary schools, secondary schools and teachers' seminaries

The compulsory school laws which operate in Norway determine the age (seven years) at which children shall enter school and the regularity of their attendance. With this in mind, it is readily understood that as a rule each class marches steadily forward, one grade each year, until the completion of the school life. As a consequence there is but little variation in the ages of pupils doing the work of any certain grade, and the proportion of pupils of normal age in the several grades is very large. In order to illustrate definitely, a concrete situation is presented in Table III, which shows the exact conditions existing at a certain time in one of their representative cities.

This table speaks for itself and needs no explanation. It is worthy of note, however, that in comparatively few instances do the ages vary more than two or three years, and that six years is the widest difference in age to be found among all the pupils of any given grade of work. Furthermore, we call attention to the fact that those above normal age in no year aggregated as much as ten per cent of the entire number in attendance. 10.1 per cent represents the entire number outside the normal age—those above plus those below—for the year 1908. During the three former years the percentage was still smaller. The reduction in numbers of pupils in the sixth and seventh grades is due in large part to the fact that so many pass from the fifth grade into the middle school.

TABLE III

Table showing the age of pupils on April 30, 1908, in the several grades, also the number in each Grade and relation to normal age.

Grade	No. of Classes	Age and year of birth.											Total	No. of Pupils of Normal Age.			Per Cent. of Normal Age.		
		6-7	7-8	8-9	9-10	10-11	11-12	12-13	13-14	14-15	15-16	16-17		Under	Norm.	Over	Under	Norm.	Over
		1902	1901	1900	1899	1898	1897	1896	1895	1894	1893	1892							
1	134	27	3047	1790	164	10							5038	27	4837	174	0.5	96.0	3.5
2	130		33	2730	1795	263	18						4839	33	4525	281	0.7	93.5	5.8
3	126			22	2564	1730	319	36	5	2			4678	22	4294	362	0.5	91.9	7.6
4	122				33	2287	1620	393	77	14	1		4425	33	3907	485	0.8	88.3	10.9
5	115					32	2009	1528	511	136	6		4222	32	3537	653	0.8	83.8	15.4
6	105					1	39	1856	1342	569	80		3878	31	3198	649	0.8	82.2	17.0
7	90							28	1582	1129	231	3	3003	28	2801	234	0.9	91.1	8.0
X[9]	2								20	22	1		43		42	1	—	97.7	2.3
T[10]	824	27	3080	4542	4556	4323	3996	3841	3537	1962	139	3	30186	206	27141	2839			
Per ct.	1908	0.1	10.2	15.1	15.1	14.3	13.2	12.7	11.7	6.5	1.1	—	—	—	—	—	0.7	89.9	9.4
	1907	0.1	11.3	15.3	15.0	13.5	13.1	12.6	11.9	6.2	1.0	—	—	—	—	—	0.8	90.9	8.3
	1906	0.1	10.9	15.5	14.6	14.0	13.4	12.5	11.6	6.6	0.8	—	—	—	—	—	0.9	91.8	7.3
	1905	0.1	11.2	15.3	14.7	14.0	13.6	12.7	11.9	6.4	0.1	—	—	—	—	—	1.1	91.7	7.2

[9] Classes requiring special individual attention.
[10] Primary schools of Kristiana exclusive of schools for abnormal children.

The same conditions of uniformity exist in the secondary schools. Having entered at the age of seven and having spent five or more years in the primary school, the pupils upon entrance to the middle school are generally twelve or more years old. In some middle schools the average age of those entering will at times be less than twelve years. This latter condition is usually due to some local situation or rule regarding age at entrance upon school work. In order to follow the age question to nearer its limits we will present Table IV.

TABLE IV

Table showing the ages of pupils in State and Communal Secondary Schools.

	Middle School				Gymnasium			
	I.	II.	III.	IV.	I.	II.	III.	Date
Trondhjem[11]	12-1[12]	13-3	14-2	15-6	16-10	17-18	18-1	9-1-06
Kristiansand[13]	12	13-5	14-2	15-2	16-3	17-7	18-3	10-1-00
Kristiansund[14]	12-7	13-5	14-8	15-5	16-2	16-9	18-4	9-1-09
Fredrikkstad[15]	12-7	13-4	14-2	15-2	15-10	16-10	17-8	7-1-08
Lillihammer[16]	12-2	13-2	14	15-3	16	16-6	18-1	7-1-06
Larvik[17]	12-2	13-3	14-2	15-1	15-10	16-10	18-2	8-1-03

Attention is called to the step from the last year in the middle school to the first year in the gymnasium. In several instances there is considerably less than a year of difference in age. This is but another illustration of the tendencies of the sifting that goes on in the natural process of selecting the fittest. Those of keenest intellect are the ones who reach a specific requirement in least time and then proceed in the pursuit of advance education. The ones sifted out are more generally those whose advance has been more difficult, or those who have lagged behind others of their own age. The absence of these tends to lower the average age in the succeeding grade. Similar conditions in emphasized form are in evidence when we study the ages of those who enter the university from year to year. While the ages of those just entering the third and final year of the gymnasium are on the average more than eighteen, the ones who enter the university the following year in September average nineteen years of age or a little less.

In addition to the tables showing the ages of pupils throughout the several grades of preparatory and secondary education, the following one is inserted to show the average age of those in attendance at four of the teachers' seminaries. The advance in age with advance of grade is not as regular here as in the other

[11] State secondary school.
[12] Age in years and months.
[13] State secondary school.
[14] State secondary school.
[15] Communal secondary schools.
[16] Communal secondary schools.
[17] Communal secondary schools.

schools.

TABLE V

Table Showing Age of Pupils in the Teachers' Seminaries at the Beginning of the Year, 1906-7.

	Average age[18] in grades.		
	I.	II.	III.
Holmestrand	19-7	21-3	22-1
Levanger	20	19-8	21-4
Hamar	19-2	20-2	21-7
Stord	19-6	19-11	21

There is not as close correspondence between age or grade and scholarship in the seminaries as we find in the other schools. The greater variation is due to several causes, among them are the following: (1) The law requires that a teacher must be at least twenty years of age.[19] (2) The previous education of those in attendance varies greatly. Many are desirous of getting as thorough and complete preparation as their circumstances admit, while others are seemingly anxious to enter on the lowest standard admissible. (3) Teachers who are eager to improve their qualifications frequently return to the seminary after a few years of teaching experience in order to complete the course and prepare for the better class of positions.

2. Comparisons with America in equipment and time spent in school

Comparisons between the educational equipment of the American youth and that of his Norwegian cousin at any given age are exceedingly difficult to make. We have not yet established any specific units or norms by which education may be measured. We can make neither definite nor satisfactory quantitative or qualitative measurements of accomplishment. However, a careful analysis of the respective courses of study, the qualification of teachers, and plans of work, supported by the testimony of those who have been teachers in both countries, seems to warrant the statement that the completion of the gymnasial course of study in Norway is comparable to the completion of the sophomore year of work in our American colleges and universities. The average age of students is about the same in both instances.

The American children spend a less portion of the year in school than do the children in Norway. While in our schools we generally have but thirty-six weeks of five days each in a year, inclusive of all regular and special holidays, the schools of Norway are in operation forty weeks of six days each, exclusive of holidays. Leaving out any consideration of holidays, the American school year usually amounts

[18] Age in years and months.

[19] Law for City Schools, Sec. 28 as revised in 1908. Law for Rural Schools, Sec. 26 as revised in 1908.

to one hundred eighty days, while in Norway they have two hundred and forty days of school. In other words, eight years of primary school and four years of high school in America represent only three-fourths as many days of instruction and study as are included in five years of primary school, four years of middle school, and three years of gymnasium in Norway. That is to say, to provide the same number of days of instruction it would take sixteen school years in America to equal twelve in Norway.

3. Specialization

The specialization which characterizes the work of the students upon entrance to the Norwegian university brings their study within much narrower limits than that of our ordinary juniors in college. Their general cultural education concludes with the taking of *artium* while ours usually continues throughout the liberal arts course in college or until the degree of Bachelor of Arts has been received. A certain amount of specialization is common among our students during the later years of their college education, but it covers a wider range than in Norway and the greater portion of it is reserved for post graduate courses. In Norway the professional studies are taken up without any preliminaries immediately upon entrance to the university. In the better professional schools of America, one, two, or three years of collegiate work is required as a preparation for entrance.

V. ORGANIZATION—RELATION TO STATE, COMMUNE, AND CITY

1. The state department and its divisions

The highest educational authority of Norway is vested in the Department of Ecclesiastical and Educational Affairs (*Kirke-og Undervisnings-Departmentet*), and the chief functionary in this department of government is a member of the King's cabinet (*Statsraad*). The work of the department is separated into two divisions, one of which supervises the ecclesiastical activities and the other the educational work of the country. This latter division is again separated into two bureaus, one having charge of primary education and the other being in control of secondary educational affairs. These bureaus perform the functions usually devolving upon such offices, the work being largely clerical. In addition there are the diocesan directors (*Stift Direktorer*) bearing the immediate responsibilities in primary education, and a state educational commission (*Undervisningsraad*) having large authority in secondary education.

Next to the department itself the school directors have authority over primary education. In fact the director has all but complete control in his territory even though the department is recognized as having the higher authority or powers. The King's cabinet appoints seven directors for the six dioceses into which the state is divided; two for the most northern, because of its greater extent, and one for each of the other five. The directors are paid by the state and are amenable only to the state, hence they exercise their powers in an endeavor to effect the best possible results educationally without fear or favor of local influences. They act independently in their respective territories and do not constitute a committee in any sense whatever.

2. Units of organization

The commission having chief oversight of secondary education consists of seven men appointed by the King's cabinet. They are chosen because of their efficiency in educational affairs without regard to the part of the country to which they belong.[20] They work always as a committee, and as experts serve the state for the general welfare of secondary education. The many privileges and duties exercised by this commission may be grouped together under the heads of inspection and supervision of secondary schools, and arrangements for having examinations. Several of the men constituting this commission are at the same time rectors of leading secondary schools in the country. In fact they are chosen because of their familiarity with and expertness in just such kind of work. When it becomes necessary to seek advice in hygienic questions a physician of recognized ability is added to the commission. His judgment and instruction are respected and adhered to very closely.

The rural communes are divided into school districts or circles (*Skolekredser*). Each district supports and maintains a primary school with at least two divisions—an infant school (*Smaaskole*) for children from seven to ten years of age, and a higher one designed for children from ten to fourteen years of age. In districts where distances are great or roadways difficult, two or more infant schools are provided.

Companies operating one or more manufacturing establishments or industrial concerns, and generally employing thirty or more laborers, are required to provide a primary school for the children of the men in their employ. When once started these schools are to be kept up unless the number of the employed is reduced below twenty. In case there are other children who desire to attend such school, they shall have the right to do so providing it does not interfere with the instruction of those for whom the school was established. In return for this the school treasury receives from the communal treasury a yearly amount proportioned to the total cost for all pupils in the school.[21]

While the law requires that instruction shall be provided six days in the week for at least twelve weeks each year, it also grants to the communes the privilege of extending the time to fifteen weeks.[22] It further provides the right to maintain six weeks additional, voluntary instruction each year.[23] These privileges are generally taken advantage of by both communes and pupils. The communes desire the extension of time for school, and the pupils are very glad of the opportunity to attend the extra time, even though their presence is not compulsory. In fact the compulsory education law has been so rigidly enforced for so long a time that reg-

[20] Some are always appointed from outside the city of Christiania.

[21] Law for Rural Schools, Sec. 42.

[22] Law for Rural Schools, Sec. 5.

[23] Law for Rural Schools, Sec. 5.

ular attendance has become habitual, and the exact provisions and requirements of the law are rarely thought of by the pupils. There is, in reality, no law requiring children to attend the schools provided by the state, but a certain amount of education is obligatory. It is mandatory that schools be maintained in all of the districts, but individual children may receive their instruction in private schools if they choose, so long as educational requirements are met from year to year. Pupils who belong to the schools are required to be in attendance regularly, and children who receive instruction elsewhere than in the state schools must meet the requirements calculated to bring them to a certain educational standard by the time they are fifteen years of age. Failure in this subjects parents, guardians, and those providing schools for children of laborers in their employ to fine or imprisonment.[24]

The work in the infant school includes or amounts to thirty lessons per week while in the higher one there are thirty-six lessons. Accordingly, the pupils in the lower grades receive a minimum of three hundred sixty lessons a year, and this number may be increased to four hundred fifty or six hundred thirty. In the higher grades they have at least four hundred thirty-two lessons a year, and if the time is extended they have five hundred forty or seven hundred fifty-six lessons a year.

3. The School Board and School Committees

Each rural commune has its own school board (*Skolestyret*) consisting of a priest; the chairman of the municipal council; one or two teachers[25] chosen by the body of teachers; as many other members (men or women) as the communal council deems it advisable to select; and the rectors of higher schools, if there be any, under the supervision and inspection of the school board.

In the towns and cities the school board consists of at least one priest[26]; a member of the city's executive council;[27] as many other members chosen for three years as the municipal council deems it advisable to select, at least half of whom must be chosen from among parents who at the time of election have children in

[24] Gathered from Law for Rural Schools, Sections 5, 15, 16, 56, 57, and 59.

[25] In communes where the number of regular teaching positions in the primary schools is fifteen or over, of which at least five are positions for females, one male and one female teacher occupying regular posts are chosen. In communes where the number of positions is under fifteen, one male or female teacher occupying a regular post is chosen. Where a male and a female teacher are to be chosen, the elections take place in separate meetings of the male and the female teachers, each selecting its representative; in the other communes election takes place in a common meeting. Election is for two years. The meetings are conducted by the chairman of the school board. Schools provided and sustained by the owners of industrial concerns within the communes may each be represented in the meetings of the school board, by an owner of such establishment, while matters pertaining to the school in which he is interested are being considered. Law for Rural Schools, Sec. 47.

[26] The law provides that there shall be on the school board a priest for each pastorate within the commune, though not to exceed three. In all cases of necessity the bishop having direction of church affairs in the locality appoints the ministerial members of the board. Their appointments are for three years.

[27] The executive board of the communal council each year elects one of its members to act on the school board for one year.

the city primary schools; one or two teachers;[28] and, wherever the school board controls higher schools, the rectors of such schools.

The members of the school board select their own chairman and act together as a committee or board. Among its more important duties are appointment of teachers and special committees, provision of course of study with specific instructions regarding its presentation, and the estimation of sums of money necessary to meet demands in the maintenance of the schools for the year. This estimate of expenses is sent by the board each year to the communal council which has charge of the dispensing of finances for the commune.

The course of study, including the plan of instruction and directions regarding the supervision of the schools as given by the board, is minutely detailed and specifically stated. It includes a list of studies to be pursued, the manner and order of their presentation, and the number of hours per week to be devoted to each subject; an outline of arrangements for entrance, promotion, and leaving examinations, with provisions for exemption therefrom wherever such is deemed advisable; all necessary arrangements for vacations; and other matters considered essential in the maintenance and carrying on of a school.

For each primary school, or for the several schools, using the same building, the board appoints a committee of inspection (*Tilsynsutvalg*). This committee consists of a member of the school board (chosen by the board), who is chairman of the committee, and three other members. These latter members are chosen in the city by the parents of children attending the school, and in the rural districts by such parents and other taxpayers. A priest appointed by church authority is added to committees serving town or city schools.

This committee of inspection exercises constant oversight of the school, keeping the board informed with reference to all matters requiring attention by that body. By the consent of the communal council this committee may have an amount provided from the school funds for its use in carrying out its work. The inspection is with special reference to the physical and moral well-being of those connected with the institution. Among the special objects of its endeavors may be enumerated the solving of all hygienic questions, regular attendance, good discipline, and proper moral conduct. The committee must also see to it that children of school age, not in attendance at the state primary schools, receive instruction in such quantity and of such quality as to meet all state requirements. In general it is an outstretched arm of the school board, feeling after the betterment of the common schools in every possible direction.

Another committee (called the school committee—*Skoleraad*) is appointed by the school board for each of the primary schools in the city. The duties of the

[28] In cities where the number of regular teaching positions is fifteen or more there are elected one male and one female teacher; and in cities where the number of regular teaching positions is less than fifteen, but at least five, one male or one female teacher. In cases where two teachers are elected, the sexes separate, each selecting its own representative; but where only one is elected they all meet together and choose one of their number. Election is for two years. The meetings are conducted by the chairman of the school board.

The above notes are from: Law for City Schools, Sec. 40.

two committees are in a way complementary. While the committee of inspection is occupied in matters external in large measure, the school committee exercises functions more pedagogical in nature, though it also has general watch care over the affairs of the school. If there be a superintendent of schools (*Skoleinspektor*), he is a member *ex officio* of the school committee, and its chairman. Under other conditions the school board designates which of the appointed members of the committee shall be its chairman. In towns where the number of teachers exceeds sixty, the school board may direct that the school committee shall consist of the superintendent and the principals of the several schools as *ex officio* members and any determined number of other teachers selected by the body of teachers. The elected members are to be male and female in proportion to their respective numbers on the teaching staff, exclusive of those who are *ex officio* members of the committee. The sexes separate into special meetings for the purpose of election, each choosing its allotted number of representatives. Election is for two years, one-half retiring each year, the first time according to lot. Members whose terms expire are required to serve longer in case of re-election. This school committee holds regular meetings, according to its own appointment, at which the members are required to be present. Furthermore, the chairman may call additional meetings in cases of necessity, and he is required to call special meetings when requested by the school board to do so. A majority vote of the members is sufficient for the passage of any proposition. While the duties of this committee are not specifically outlined, it is intended that its work shall concern chiefly the internal workings of the schools. Its functions are mainly pedagogical in character as already stated and as evidenced in the following provisions in the law. "The school board shall permit the school committee to voice its opinions in every affair which concerns: (1) the general supervision of primary schools, (2) general provisions concerning regulations and discipline, and (3) text books and outlines of instruction." In addition the committee is required to express itself regarding any matter relating to the good of the school when asked by the board for advice.

4. City superintendent (Inspector) and ward principles (Overlaererer)

The school board may also order that there be a teachers' commission (*Laererraad*) for each school or for the several schools using the same buildings, consisting of the teachers in the school. The chairman of this committee is the superintendent of schools, a school principal, or other member, according to the determination of the board. The duties devolving upon this commission are in each case outlined by the board.

The superintendent of schools (*Skoleinspektor*) has general direction of all the primary schools in the city system. His duties are similar to those of the superintendent in American towns and cities. He takes the lead in directing the policies of the schools and exercises large powers in making them efficient. He is provided with well-equipped offices, generally in one of the school buildings, where he and his clerks, supplied by the school board, do the greater portion of their work.

A principal or headmaster (*Overlaerer*) is generally placed in charge of each school. His duties are comparable to those performed by ward principals in the United States. While the superintendent is the superior officer and exercises general control and authority, the principal has immediate charge of the work of the school. He controls its activities in harmony with and under the direction of the superintendent, consulting the wishes of the higher official and respecting his opinions. The superintendent recognizes that for the one in immediate charge of a school to have his hands tied or his liberties too circumscribed means the hampering of the work; hence, he gives to the principals working under him wide latitude in carrying out their ideas. For example, if the principal is a believer in coeducation or, on the other hand, a staunch advocate of segregation of the sexes for instructional purposes, he is usually privileged to carry his policy into execution in his school, even though the views of the superintendent are not wholly in accord therewith. Throughout their work they seek each other's counsel and advice, and cooperate successfully.

5. Private citizens a factor

The private citizen in Norway plays only an indirect part in school affairs, yet his interests are conserved in various ways. The local pastor, who is a member *ex officio* of the school board, generally guards the interests of the masses. His influence and vote may be regarded usually as a reflection of the popular mind. The chairman of the municipal council, who also is a member of the board by virtue of his position, is indirectly the choice of the people. The teacher or teachers chosen to occupy on the school board nearly always work in harmony with the public will. The committee of inspection has a majority of its members chosen directly by vote of the people immediately concerned. The press is free and educational movements are continually discussed in the leading papers. Further than this, educational affairs are common topics of conversation, being talked of on all occasions under various circumstances and conditions. It may be said to their credit that those discussing these subjects do so intelligently and critically. The masses are alive to the educational situation, are intensely interested in their schools, and are acquainted with the provisions of the law concerning them. The people being so democratic in tendency and so very frank in the expression of their feelings and opinions, naturally reflect public sentiment; which because of being understood has more weight and is correspondingly a greater factor in legislative activities.

6. Financial support of schools

The primary schools receive their financial support from the state, county, and commune. The state provides for city schools one-third of straight salaries, which range between twelve hundred and fourteen hundred crowns for men, and between eight hundred and nine hundred crowns for women; two-thirds of additional salary paid because of long service to the limit of eight hundred crowns per year for men and five hundred crowns per year for women; and one-third of salaries paid for positions requiring only part time, for teaching by the hour, and for teaching in continuation schools. In certain cases where the treasuries are depleted the state treasury furnishes as high as forty-five per cent of teachers' salaries within the fixed limits mentioned above. In the rural communes the grant received from the state amounts to forty-five per cent of the teachers' salaries, and where finances are low this amount may be increased to sixty per cent. The amount of this state grant is figured on the basis of salaries that do not exceed twenty-four crowns per week in the second or higher division, and nineteen crowns in the first or infant division of the primary school, except in the county of Finnmarken where the bases may be respectively twenty-eight crowns and twenty-two crowns per week.

In each county (*Amt*) the county council provides funds for the following purposes: raising teachers' salaries in case of long service, erecting school buildings, supplying teachers' homes, paying substitute teachers, purchasing apparatus, relieving communes and municipalities where school expenses are disproportionately high, and maintaining continuation and artisan schools. Whatever is required to defray the expenses of the primary schools, in addition to state and county grants, tuition, receipts from school lands or holdings, etc., is furnished by the commune or municipality through its council.

The secondary schools are either state or communal. The state schools are provided with grounds, buildings, and equipment by the communes in which they are located; the remaining expenses are met by state grants, tuition fees, etc. The expense of maintaining communal schools falls largely upon the communes. The state furnishes one-third of the salaries in both classes of schools, and all additional amounts paid to teachers because of long service. While most of the secondary schools charge regular tuition fees, all of them have funds which supply free scholarships to a number of pupils each year. In some communes they have been able already to provide free middle schools, and it appears at least possible that all state and communal schools may sometime be free. The aim in financing the school system is to equalize the burden of expense as far as possible, and to recognize, at the same time, the efforts of those directly concerned. In order to obtain the best results, authority has been strongly centralized; school boards, communal and county councils, and state officials exercise large discretionary powers.

VI. BUILDINGS AND GROUNDS

1. General character of buildings

The school buildings of Norway are justly reputed to be the most magnificent, best located, and finest edifices of the country. They are built of substantial materials according to attractive architectural designs, and are provided with liberal equipment. The larger buildings are usually constructed of stone, brick and stone, or brick and cement; while the smaller ones are built of lumber and stone. In the erection of buildings, great care is exercised to make them spacious and permanent. All materials used are selected because of their durability and suitability to purpose. In order to guarantee the best hygienic conditions, the law provides that buildings must meet the approval of experts in hygiene before they can be used for school purposes. This means that the services of these experts must be secured in getting out designs for school buildings, whether in the erection of new or the remodeling of old ones.

2. Equipment

The school buildings are heated by furnaces or stoves. The newer ones are modern in every respect and, of course, have excellent heating systems. Those which have done service for several decades are usually heated by stoves.

The buildings are divided into rooms in such a manner that the daylight nearly always enters from the left or the rear of the pupils when they are seated at their desks. This rule is disregarded only in rare cases. During the short days of winter it is essential to provide artificial light. In cities and large towns they use electricity for lighting the school buildings; in the country or in small towns, where the municipalities do not maintain any central lighting plant, various devices are installed. Sometimes gasoline is used and again ordinary oil lamps are common. An abundance of light of the best procurable quality is generally provided.

Besides admitting light the outside windows are of use in providing ventilation for the school rooms. They are opened wide during intermissions between classes, so that when the children come in from their exercise on the play grounds they enter an atmosphere nearly as pure and fresh as that out of doors. In addition, many schoolhouses, especially those built recently, have regular ventilating devices.

The class room furniture in Norway, like that used in many other European schools, is about as primitive in design and lacking in attractiveness as anything found in the whole country. Its evolution surely has been greatly retarded. In each room there is a small platform high enough to enable the instructor to see all his pupils with ease. On this platform is a desk and a high chair in which the teacher sits most of the time while giving instruction.

The pupils' seats and desks are made of heavy lumber and attached to a common base. This makes them clumsy, and they appear very queer to one accustomed to the better designs now in use in some countries. Those of recent make are for but one pupil, though older ones, some of which are still in use, accommodate three or four. In construction the seat is generally a solid flat bench with a low back. The desk has a slightly sloping top, a small inconvenient shelf for books, and a receptacle for pencils, pens, rulers, and other articles used by school children. The Norwegians deserve commendation for the care exercised in the arrangement of seats and desks. The distance and proportion between them are regulated according to scientific principles looking to the physical welfare of the occupants. The bodily posture of children in school determines in large measure what it will be out of school. Far too little attention has been given the physical side of education, and one of the important problems in connection therewith is the proper construction of schoolroom furniture.

In the smaller buildings, classrooms have commodious cupboards for apparatus (maps, charts, globes, plates, etc.), and various things with which the children work (sewing materials, exercise books, etc.). While they have a liberal supply of excellent illustrative material and teaching apparatus and the best of facilities for storing it, mechanical appliances for its display and devices for its convenient use are woefully lacking. Maps and charts are held in the hand or hung on a nail or other fixture in the room; while globes and the like are placed on chairs or improvised stands. In general the apparatus is awkward to manipulate and as a result much of its value is lost.

Blackboards of proper size are very rare in the schools of Norway. As a rule the board is about three by five feet in size and fastened to a clumsy easel which elevates it so high that it is out of reach of the pupils. To enable the children to use such a board a small platform is provided. The child mounts the platform by means of a few steps and there stands and does his blackboard work. In only one instance did the writer during his visits to the schools find what appeared to him to be an adequate amount of blackboard space. This exceptional condition was in one of the primary schools where special equipment was installed for the instruction of children below normal intelligence. The ample provision of blackboard here is proof of a recognition of its value, and the situation may also be regarded as an indictment against the prevalent neglect in this line.

School room decorations are not as prominent as might be expected. Despite the facts that the whole of Norway is picturesque, that her artists are quite numerous, and that the masses of her people are more than ordinarily appreciative of the finer phases of life, very few paintings or pieces of sculpture adorn her schools. True, exceptions as to this rule of scant provision of the artistic may be found; but, as in all countries, they quite generally fail to appreciate the educative values of art.

While, traditionally at least, the study and recitation rooms have been considered of prime and greatest importance in school buildings, there are others, accessory to them, which in their effects are productive of quite as good results. Among them may be mentioned: offices, teachers' rooms, libraries, laboratories, and other rooms for special purposes. Some of these are not provided in all schools, but commonly all of them are found in the city school buildings.

The offices for rectors, inspectors, head masters, etc., are admirably arranged and handsomely appointed. They are provided with desks, cabinets, chairs, settees, tables, and other furnishings which add to convenience and comfort. The rooms for teachers are equipped and furnished in a way just as suitable to their purpose. In these they spend their vacant periods in study, reading, or in leisure, according to their choice. Here, too, officers and teachers are served with luncheons in the middle of forenoon and afternoon sessions.

There are libraries in nearly all school buildings. While many of them are small some are of large consequence. The one in the Christiania Cathedral School numbers thirty thousand volumes. This is one of the oldest and perhaps the largest library in any school of the country, and it is regarded with considerable justifiable pride.

The laboratories are furnished in harmony with their traditional plan of instruction. Instead of having a supply of apparatus so that most or all of the pupils may be occupied simultaneously in laboratory experimentation, they have but one set of instruments. However, they do furnish liberal quantities of materials for laboratory experimentation. The teacher is the chief operator, one or two pupils assist in the work, and the other members of the class are onlookers.

Where domestic arts are taught, rooms are fitted up especially for the purpose. Stoves, cooking utensils, and many other necessary articles are at hand ready for use. The efficiency of the work is in no wise hindered by lack of supplies. In many instances teachers go themselves to the markets and purchase provisions needed for the day. An earnest effort is made to combine theory and practice in proportions suitable to obtaining the best possible results.

Some of the larger buildings have special rooms for the storing of apparatus and illustrative materials (*Anskuelsesmidler*). Racks, cupboards, cabinets, drawers, cases, and the like provide convenient means for preserving these supplies and of rendering them easily accessible. Gymnastic halls and lunch rooms will be discussed in another section.

3. Playgrounds

The playgrounds are generally small, but some of the schools have, in addition to the grounds immediately surrounding the buildings, athletic parks of considerable proportions. The grounds about the school buildings are arranged with a view of securing from them maximum returns. They are enclosed by high board or wire fence, or by stone or brick and cement walls. A heavy coating of gravel is usually placed on the ground in order to avoid the growth of vegetation or an accumulation of dust. "Keep off the grass" signs are not in evidence, for rarely do they attempt to have grassy lawns.

They recognize the need and value of physical exercise in the open, and provide means for it in connection with every school. It is specifically required that all pupils go on to the playgrounds during the intermissions (*fri Krarterer*) which come between all lessons. While the children are at play one or more of the teachers are detailed to supervise the grounds, while others are to patrol the hallways. Large roofs are put up under which the children play when the weather is not favorable to being in the open. On rare occasions when the weather is bitter, pupils may be permitted to remain indoors. Children whose health is extremely delicate are dealt with in leniency, and some of them are permitted to remain inside regularly.

4. Homes for principals and teachers

Near to the school buildings, generally on a corner of the grounds, homes are provided for the head master or principal and the janitor (*Vagtmester*). Sometimes the janitor and his family live in an apartment in the school building. Generally, however, a double house is erected, one part for the principal and the other for the janitor. These homes are furnished rent free to these men.

Teachers in rural districts, as a rule, are supplied with a house and sufficient ground for garden and the pasturage of two or three cows. These provisions materially reduce living expenses, and, in a way, recompense for the low salaries received. In one rural school the writer found three hundred and fifty pupils taught in two divisions—forenoon and afternoon sessions—by six teachers. The principal had been in charge of the school forty-three years. One portion of the school building provided a residence for him and his family. They had a small garden; a fruit orchard; a few acres of land for pasturage and hay; and a barn and sheds for cow, pig, and chickens. There are many similar situations throughout the country. This particular one lay just outside a small city, and this fact accounts in part for the large number of pupils in attendance.

As a rule the homes for rural school teachers compare very favorably with the better class of homes in the surrounding neighborhood. They have sufficient room, are comfortable, and generally satisfy the occupants. The majority of rural teachers have such homes provided, though only a few city teachers enjoy this favor. In 1905, two thousand, eight hundred and twenty-six rural teachers had homes furnished them free of cost.

VII. GENERAL FEATURES OF INNER ORGANIZATION

1. The teaching staff

Most of the teachers in the rural primary schools are men, while the majority of them in the city are women. During the year 1907 there were four thousand, one hundred and twenty-three male and one thousand, four hundred and seven female teachers occupying regular positions in the rural schools, and in the city their numbers were respectively eight hundred and twenty-eight and one thousand, six hundred and six. Although the law makes no requirements as to sex, except that in city schools there must be at least one master and one governess, there are certain forces operative which almost equal edicts of law. Traditionally, teachers in the rural schools are men and, as previously stated, homes are provided for them and their families. Appointments to teaching positions are permanent. Teachers remain in their places until death removes them or until they choose to retire on pension, which is, all too often, long after they pass the time of their efficiency. It is difficult to break with the old customs and hence the entrance of women teachers into the rural school positions has been slow. In the cities the conditions are different. There only a small percentage of the teachers have homes furnished them, the number of teaching positions without supervising responsibility is large, and the salaries paid to women are lower than those paid to men. As a consequence the female teachers have found easy entrance into the city schools, and at present they outnumber the men two to one. Women have been teaching since 1869, and the people are convinced that their ability as teachers is equal to that of the sterner sex.

2. Plan of instruction

In the secondary schools, also, the majority of the instructors are men. In the gymnasia practically all of them are men, but in the middle schools there are many women teachers. Even though the Norwegians recognize woman's ingenuity and efficiency in teaching small children, they have not yet become converted to the idea that she is man's equal in the more advanced educational fields. It seems probable that tradition is the chief hindrance to the entrance of women into teaching positions in the gymnasia.

In their plan of instruction there is much to commend and some things to criticise. The teachers do a large amount of teaching, but they also provide opportunity for the children to do a great deal on their own initiative, so that they too may know the joy of discovery and feel the triumph of mastery. The Norwegian pedagogue uses the recitation period, nearly always fifty minutes, in an endeavor to impart information, both directly and indirectly; directly by straightforward giving, and indirectly through cooperative mental activities. While they feel the importance of direct instruction, they see, also, the advantage in shifting a part of the responsibility to the pupils. They recognize the fact that the child has ability, and that by himself he is capable of finding and recognizing problems, and of working them out to satisfying conclusions. They appreciate that even a small child is able to carry out many educative activities with a minimum of direction from the teacher, and that the development which comes from this self-direction and initiative is one of the most valuable ends of education. The intent is that the class period shall be devoted to exercises which will furnish information and, at the same time, make the children independent and able to direct themselves.

Though the ideals and aims are excellent, the means for attaining them are not the best. There is a certain inherited aloofness on the part of the instructor which robs both teacher and pupils of some of the values which come from closer association. During the recitation hour the teacher nearly always occupies the high chair on the elevated platform, except while using the blackboard or doing other demonstrational work. My observations convince me that the teachers, especially the men, do not get down and work among and with the children as much as seems essential to the accomplishment of the greatest good.

Now the discipline and character of recitations also deserve attention. When a pupil is called upon to recite, he is expected to pass to the aisle and there stand erect until the recitation is completed. Only in rare cases are children allowed to sit while reciting. I have seen children only eleven or twelve years of age called to the front of the room to analyze and develop a problem. The smallest children are required to give only short answers to questions, but responses rapidly increase in length, as age advances, until they amount to minute and extended discussions of topics. Recitations lasting ten to fifteen minutes are not uncommon, and the children become quite expert in the relation of facts and in the development of problems presented. This method of procedure is perhaps all right for a certain class of children, but timid boys and girls are sometimes embarrassed to the extent that they are unable to do credit to themselves, their teachers, or the lessons. On one occasion I saw a boy who was so frightened in an attempt to stand and recite, being required at the same time to look into the face of a complaining teacher, that he was unable to say anything whatever. The teacher, a man of advanced age, finally awoke to the situation, and placing his hand on the boy's head, talked to him about the lesson until he calmed the lad's fears and obtained a very satisfactory response from him.

3. Gymnastics

In addition to classroom activities connected with mental growth, considerable work is done looking to physical development. Gymnastic exercise is required of all children in primary and secondary schools, excepting those in first and second grades and a few who are physically disqualified for it. To provide for this work, the city schools furnish large halls with excellent equipment, and special teachers to give instruction. A Swedish system of gymnastics is in vogue throughout the country. There seems to be no criticism against the system, and the benefits testify emphatically to its efficiency. The apparatus is simple and inexpensive, but the variety of movements and the numberless combinations of them seem to answer every demand.

4. Lunches

Certain conditions and customs prevailing in Norway make it necessary to serve lunches at the school buildings. The morning sessions are long and the dinner hour is far later than noon—generally two or three o'clock. Furthermore, many children of poor parentage come to school underfed. Opportunity to obtain a light lunch of nourishing food and a warm drink at about 10:30 or 11 o'clock is an appreciated necessity. Hence most buildings have lunch rooms arranged and equipped according to local demands. Here, in the secondary schools, the family of the janitor furnishes rolls, buns, cakes, cocoa, coffee, milk, etc., at a reasonable rate. As stated before, the teachers have lunches served in their own rooms. Some cities provide children in the primary schools with one meal of wholesome food each day of school during the winter months—generally from the middle of October until the first of May. This is free to the needy children, and others obtain it at first cost.

In Christiania they have a central kitchen from which the city primary schools receive supplies. This kitchen has a capacity for steam cooking, ten thousand liters at a time. Only the best food is purchased. This is carefully prepared and delivered every day in tightly sealed cans to the several schools where it is served hot. The maintenance of this kitchen is in answer to recommendations made by a committee, appointed by the school board, after visiting various similar European institutions and studying carefully into their operations. In equipment, management, and good results it is not surpassed in any city in Europe or America. In some of the schools, hundreds of free meals are dispensed every day throughout the long winter. During the year 1908-1909, from October 19, 1908, to April 30, 1909, (one hundred and thirty-two days), the Christiania central kitchen furnished 616,821 free meals and 77,733 meals which were paid for by children in the schools. This work stands as a testimonial to the beneficence of the people whose circumstances enable them to maintain it.

5. School discipline

The discipline of the school borders on the military order. The pupils form in line and march in passing to and from classrooms and playgrounds. While the work of instruction proceeds strict discipline is maintained. Before entering a classroom where a recitation is in progress, one invariably knocks at the door, whoever he is and whatever his errand, and by the time he enters teacher and pupils are on their feet. Turning to the one entering, they bow and continue to face him until he is seated, which is a signal to them to sit. Should the visitor withdraw before the class is dismissed, the pupils again rise to their feet and bow him out; but, if he remains until they are dismissed, they bow to him before taking their departure. Every activity indoors and out of doors is closely supervised, and the control exercised over the pupils is praiseworthy.

6. Attendance

Attendance at school is regular in all grades. When children are absent for any reason the case is inquired into without delay, and, unless satisfactory excuse or explanation is forthcoming, the truant officers are on hand to enforce regulations. Failure to comply with the laws regarding absence from school, subjects parents or guardians of children to a fine of from one to twenty-five crowns.[29] Very rarely is an enforcement of these laws necessary, for the people are generally law-abiding and peace-loving. Being eager for development, they gladly comply with educational provisions without any compulsion, and regularity in attendance is the universal practice. Sickness is perhaps the most common excuse given for absence and, since excellent health is characteristic of the people, this is infrequent.

7. Health

Pupils are nearly always healthy, vigorous, and robust. One of the chief points calling attention to this is the rarity of cases where glasses are worn. In visiting schools I noticed that spectacled children were very few. I was at first inclined to criticise what I interpreted to be neglect of the eyes, but soon found that eyesight, as well as the general health of the children, was being carefully guarded. Every school has its physician whose duty it is to regulate sanitation and to remedy physical defects of children. I ascertained that in some schools special examinations had been conducted for the testing of eyesight, and results showed that very few of the pupils were under the necessity of wearing glasses. Among the causes contributing to this favorable situation may be mentioned a healthful climate, regular drill in gymnastics, proper lighting of school rooms, good ventilation, physical exercise in the open between successive classes, and, in general, the maintenance of a high state of physical vigor. The Norse take justifiable pride in their physical development, and they pay considerable attention to this phase of education. Consequently the children are able to attack the strenuous activities of school life with vim, and mastery of the course of study is not a hardship.

[29] Law for Rural Schools, Sec. 15. A crown is equal to about twenty-seven cents.

CHAPTER II

TEACHERS

I. QUALIFICATIONS AND CERTIFICATION OF TEACHERS

1. General situation and tendencies

Teaching is a profession in Norway. Those following it have chosen it as their life work. The people thus engaged deserve and receive the recognition, confidence, and esteem of the masses, and they maintain the dignity of their calling. As a class they rank high educationally, morally, and professionally. With the advance in social ideals it has been necessary to raise the standards of preparation for teaching, and, as the years pass, further changes will be required. For a long time, professional training has been demanded of every appointee to a teaching position, and indications point to a rapid development of the quality of this training until every resource is operative.

2. Special teachers

The law requires that to be eligible for appointment to a regular teaching position in the secondary schools (middle school and gymnasium), one must have had a course in the university and special training provided in the pedagogical seminary. This means that the candidate has completed: (1) the twelve years of work in the primary and secondary schools, where a wide range of instruction and general culture are provided; (2) a course in the university (four to seven years in length), devoted to exhaustive research in the particular branches of study which are subsequently to be taught; and (3) the course of training given in the pedagogical seminary.

It is the aim and function of this seminary to provide for the university graduates who are to become teachers the most practical and complete professional training possible within the limits of time (six months). It is readily evident that excellence in educational equipment and intelligent insight into the business of teaching are among the accomplishments of the profession. In fact, mastery of the field to be taught and professional training in its presentation are requisites.

The certificates or diplomas issued upon completion of the preparatory work just outlined are the only credentials required of the Norwegian teachers. Being issued by the state they have a standard of value which is uniform, recognized, and honored throughout the realm. Without these papers it would be folly to seek appointment to a fixed (permanent) post.

Besides the regular corps of instructors occupying on full time in the general lines of instruction, there are many special teachers devoting their energies along particular lines of work, such as home economics, drawing, music, gymnastics, and manual training; and still others who teach some of the regular branches of study only part time, whose positions are not permanent. Special preparation is required in order to obtain positions in these specific lines of work.

II. TRAINING OF TEACHERS

1. Introductory

Norway early recognized the value of specific training for the work of the teacher. The experiences of other nations served as object lessons illustrating the good coming from the services of properly equipped teachers and the dangers of proceeding without such. The state was eager to lay substantial foundations, to conserve and develop every resource, to build permanently and economically, and to profit by the experiences of other systems. Consequently, the people moved forward in a conservative manner and planned for the future as well as for immediate needs.

Utilizing the strong points of other systems and adapting them to local conditions, the state established six teachers' seminaries, locating one in each of the six dioceses into which the country is divided, so that they would be within easy access of the people attending them. Besides these state seminaries, four private institutions, having almost identical functions, have been established and are flourishing. The private seminaries are located at vantage points not too close to the State Schools yet where they will be within reach of a large number of people. The favorable location of these schools makes it possible for a large number of the attendants to live in their own homes, while the large majority need be but a short distance from their homes.

The work of the teachers' seminaries is, of course, to provide special preparation for teaching in the schools throughout the nation. Their curricula are similar to those used in the secondary schools. The chief point of difference between them is the attitude taken toward the subjects of instruction. In the secondary schools the aim is general and in a large measure cultural, while in the seminaries the attempt is always to present the lesson or subjects of instruction in such a manner that the pupils shall get both intellectual development and the correct method of presentation. It is the intent that this experience shall help to qualify for the successful teaching of the subjects studied. The work corresponds closely with that done in the normal schools of America or similar teachers' schools in other lands.

It is everywhere true that teachers teach as they have been taught. The principle of imitation is illustrated clearly every day in every school room. Teachers, like pupils, follow example more closely than precept. Providing schools designed to fit people for the teaching profession have ideal teachers, they will be able to turn out from year to year groups of teachers, who, imitating their masters, both in the application of scientific principles of method and in the exercise of individuality, will in turn become ideal teachers. If the curriculum and teaching of the training college are rich and varied, its products will be characterized by efficiency and resourcefulness. On the contrary, should the work of the school be narrow because of a cramped curriculum, or on account of biased and shrunken ideals of the faculty, the results will be unsatisfactory. The teachers who go out from such an institution will be unequal to the tasks awaiting them—they will be unable to meet the situation in the educational field.

Since it is a chief occupation of the training school to instill methods of presentation, there is great danger of becoming mechanical, machine-made, or stilted in one way or another. Quite the opposite must be the nature and work of the teacher. The teacher should be able to come down from the high platform and cooperate with the children; to find the individual child and his interests and, in a genuinely sympathetic spirit, to direct those interests; to discard set rules, hard and fast lines, and pet theories; and to open up to each child a vision of the fields before. In order to do these things the instructor must be thoroughly familiar with child life: its nature, mental and physical make-up, processes of development, conditions of growth and activity, instincts, and hopes. He must also cherish and manifest a sympathetic attitude towards youthful tendencies and aspirations, and be able to inspire the pupils to noble purposes.

2. Seminaries—establishment and work

The seminaries of Norway, like those of other nations, fall short of some of the conditions of excellence that we yearn for. They do not include a sufficient amount of professional training nor is that which is provided always the ideal type. Nevertheless, an earnest effort is being put forth to approach these higher conditions as rapidly as possible. The course of three years, besides furnishing a valuable fund of instruction, provides a large amount of work in observation and extensive experience in teaching. The training in observation generally consists of work in connection with the state schools (primary and secondary) in the immediate vicinity of the seminary. Into these state schools the seminary pupils are permitted to go and observe the teaching of the regularly employed instructors as they present the different subjects in the curriculum. After having observed teaching for some time and having carefully discussed class room procedure with their own teachers, they are required to specially prepare and present some lessons under the close, yet sympathetic scrutiny and supervision of their masters. As time passes, more and more of this practice teaching is assigned until proficiency is attained in the presentation of subjects to be taught in subsequent years. While these schools do not incorporate into their activities all things that seem important, it must be said to their credit that they have done a great service in qualifying teachers for the class of instruction which has already raised the masses to their present place of literary distinction.

Besides the institutions providing teachers' training above referred to, there was established in 1907 the Pedagogical seminary. This seminary is affiliated with the university in Christiania but is not an organic part of it. It was founded by act of the Stortbing and is supported by the state. The function of the Pedagogical Seminary is to provide professional training of an especially practical type for graduates of the university who intend to make teaching their profession. The length of the course is six months. Instruction and training provided in this institution includes: (1) lectures in hygiene, psychology, history of education, and principles of education; (2) observation of class instruction by masters, whose teaching is the highest representation of the art in the city; (3) discussions, formal and informal, general and analytic, with the headmaster of the seminary concerning methods of instruction, class conduct, and school management; and (4) practice teaching under the supervision of masters whose criticisms are given in such frank and sympathetic manner as to make them invaluable.

As a rule, those trained in the teachers' seminaries are employed in the primary schools. The students who avail themselves of the advantages of a university education and follow it by the training provided in the Pedagogical Seminary generally become teachers in the secondary schools. The seminary training in general is of such character that it may be put into use immediately upon entrance into the work of teaching. It also renders vital and usable for purposes of instruction the information and intellectual development gained during the long-continued and intensive schooling preceding such training.

III. TEACHERS' OFFICIAL TITLES

1. In the several schools—significance

Throughout the school system of Norway teachers are given titles according to the nature of the positions occupied. In the primary school the man who does the supervising work (in America known as superintendent) is called the *Inspektor*; the head teacher or principal is termed the *Overlaerer*; and the other teachers, male and female, are spoken of respectively as *Laerer* and *Laererinde*. In the middle school and gymnasium the titles are *Rektor*, *Overlaerer*, and *Adjunkt*. The *Rektor* has the supervisory work and some teaching to do; the *Overlaerer* is one of the principal teachers who has been given the title and ranking, chiefly because of fitness and long service; and the *Adjunkt* is a regular teacher who has served the school for five years or more and has received permanent appointment.

Titles do not correspond strictly to educational equipment nor do they depend wholly upon term of service, though both of these may be and generally are contributory factors. For example: positions in the middle schools and gymnasia are open only to those who have certain educational fitness; the teachers with especially strong qualifications and superior ability are the ones most liable to receive early promotion to the higher class positions; and, when promotions are made, the persons who have taught for a long time enjoy some advantage over those with but slight experience. Titles correspond more definitely to classes of positions occupied than to any other thing that can be named. When an individual is appointed to a position carrying a title, that designation is invariably used in connection with his name. He is no longer John Johnson or Herr Johnson, but *Rektor* Johnson, *Overlaerer* Johnson, *Inspektor* Johnson, etc.

IV. TEACHERS' TENURE OF OFFICE

1. Positions—Permanent and temporary

The teacher's tenure of office in Norway is very different from what we are accustomed to in America. Positions are of two kinds—permanent and temporary. Nearly all appointments in the past have been to permanent posts. This means that the individual occupies his place without molestation or any hint of insecurity until he chooses to resign or until he reaches the age of retirement.[30] Some appointments now are to temporary positions though generally they lead to permanent ones. Rarely, if ever, does a person who makes reasonable success in a temporary position fail to secure an appointment to a permanent post.

Permanency in position has a number of well-recognized advantages. Security of situation gives to the teacher a release from the uncertainty which constantly harasses the minds of so many where frequent change of position is the rule. A lasting appointment enables one to get a firm grasp on the local situation, and to utilize without waste all the momentum accumulated while occupying in a particular place. Furthermore, the teacher who feels settled in a position is able to establish a home, and to become identified with the community and its interest.

Since teachers continue for so long a time in a position, they and their pupils become as well acquainted with each other as with members of a common family. It is interesting to note how minutely a teacher knows the daily life and habits of his pupils. While the relations are not always the most congenial, they are known to be practically inevitable and impossible of escape so they each make the best of the situation and get the most out of it.

Again, when children know that it will be their lot to come under the tuition of a certain instructor who occupies a permanent post under state appointment, they work faithfully and usually eliminate any criticising attitude. In fact, long terms of service tend to inhibit the criticisms of both children and parents which sometimes attend teachers who occupy positions but for a short time. The situation conduces to a condition of harmony and cooperative activity. The children instinctively feel the authority of the teacher. They know that he has the support of local and state authorities, and that they will cooperate with him in carrying forward his projects. The teacher, in turn, recognizes his responsibilities in the premises and endeavors to occupy acceptably.

Now it is just as true that there are some disadvantages to permanency of positions. Teachers are apt to become non-progressive and in some cases, little more than fixtures. Change of environment stimulates progress and development. Variety in teaching experience broadens the capabilities and increases the usefulness of teachers. In addition, children need the touch and influence of many lives. They receive greater inspiration because of coming in contact with the personality

[30] Law for Secondary Schools, Sec. 33.

of a large number of teachers. However, too frequent change is wasteful. It dissipates the energy of teachers and breaks the continuity of the work of the children. Where the permanency of positions is absolutely uncertain, the teaching profession is transitory and dwindling. Only a few remain for long time in the work under such conditions. Many efficient school men leave the profession annually because of this discouragement.

At present, the feeling appears to be general that permanency in position should be conditioned upon improvement in efficiency. Evidently a recognition of this principle is a basic cause underlying the increase in number of appointments to temporary teaching positions. This procedure affords an excellent opportunity for weeding out the unfit. At the same time it acts as a spur inducing growth and development. Progressive tendencies, along with other qualifications, are regarded necessary to appointment even to temporary posts, and, as implied before, success in such positions is a prerequisite to appointment to permanent ones.

2. Comparisons with conditions in America

In America, teacher's tenure of office is very short. Each year there are many changes in the personnel of teachers throughout the country. Here we have the extreme of uncertainty, while in Norway they go to the limits of certainty in teaching positions. Both these extremes are unfortunate. Could a golden mean be reached which would include proper incentives to and recognition of continuous self-improvement and a reasonable sense of security in permanent occupation, the profession would call into its ranks a large and more efficient body of men and women, and the schools would make greater and more substantial progress. In order to illustrate the permanency of positions in Norway Table VI has been arranged.

3. Changes in teaching staff (with tables)

It is immediately apparent that the changes in the body of teachers are rare. It is also evident that nearly all who leave the profession do so on legitimate grounds. A few changes result from transfers in position, a large per cent of withdrawals are retirements after extended periods of service, and many vacancies are due to death. Fifty per cent or more of the women who retire do so on account of marrying, a few die at their posts, and many retire on pensions. Very few of the women teachers retire to enter other lines of work. While the table does not indicate how much longer than thirty years some teachers remain in the service, it may be added here that examples are not rare where individuals continue teaching for more than half a century. In most cases teachers occupy the same position throughout their teaching experience.

TABLE VI

Table indicating Retirement from Teaching Staff and Reasons for Retirement.

Year	1890		1895		1900		1905	
Sex	Male	Female	Male	Female	Male	Female	Male	Female
Total number of positions	3941	1187	4402	2116	4670	2613	4865	2885
Total number leaving	117	17	88	22	106	89	110	90
Vacated after a period service from								
1 to 10 years	19	11	21	13	24	65	20	53
10 to 20 years	26	4	10	7	10	13	19	19
20 to 30 years	38	1	18		16	5	13	10
Over 30 years	34	1	39	2	56	6	58	8
Reasons for leaving								
Death	30	1	24	2	30	6	32	11
Retirement on pension	39	3	48	3	53	21	59	22
Change in position	9				3	2	4	4
Marriage		9		11		47		48
Various others	39	4	16	6	20	13	15	5

V. TEACHERS' SALARIES

1. General statement

2. Additional benefits

The salaries received by teachers do not average high in Norway. Many provisions are made, however, for the reduction of their living expenses. All those who serve the school authorities in Norway receive certain benefits appertaining to the positions they hold. For example: There is advance in salaries on promotions and after specified periods of service; teachers are exempt from expense incident to particular offices; school authorities send all official communications through the mail free of postage; teachers receive pensions on retirement from positions; the rural school teachers frequently receive, in addition to their salary, a house to live in and sufficient land for the pasturage of two or three cows, and in towns and cities some of the teachers have homes provided, or are allowed a certain amount per year for living expenses. These and similar concessions and provisions are extended to the teachers according to enactments of the state, individual communes, or municipalities. Generally, a regular schedule is made out by which salaries are governed. Table VII indicates the salaries for different positions in eight cities of Norway:

3. Schedules (with tables)

The table is made up from the salary schedules of typical cities of various sizes. The values are in *kroner* (one *krone* is practically the equivalent of twenty-seven cents in United States money). We note that salaries are medium in the beginning, and that they increase at regular intervals until certain limits are reached. When we consider these limiting salaries, the long service generally rendered at the highest rate, certainty of position, and the pension to be received upon retirement, we are prone to admit that the advantages are not altogether in favor of the higher salaries paid in our American schools. True, the American teacher generally receives larger returns in dollars and cents, but the Norwegian pedagogue is less mercenary than his American cousin. He is satisfied when his wants and those of his family are liberally provided for. His life is not strenuous. It is happy and filled with the joys of service and the companionship of youthful souls. Anxieties are in large measure overcome by the assurance that the state will provide necessities when the time for retirement comes. Pensions are graduated according to individual necessity as well as with reference to position, term of service, and salary at the time of retirement.

TABLE VII

Schedule of Salaries paid to Teachers in the Primary Schools of eight cities in Norway.[31]

			Salary After (in Kr.)						
City	Position	Begin'ng Salary	3 yrs.	5 yrs.	6 yrs.	9 yrs.	10 yrs.	12 yrs.	15 yrs.
1. Christiania	Overlaerer	3000	3400		3700	4000			
	Laerer, h.g.	3000							
	Laerer, l.g.	1600	1800		2100	2400		2700	3000
	Laererinde, h.g.	1700							
	Laererinde, l.g.	1100	1200		1300	1400		1500	1700
2. Fredrikshald	Laerer, h.g.	2200							
	Laerer, l.g.	1300	1450		1650	1750		1900	2000
	Laererinde, h.g.	1250							
	Laererinde, l.g.	950	1000		1050	1100		1150	
3. Sarpsborg	Laerer, h.g.	1800	2000						
	Laerer, l.g.	1200	1400		1600	1700		1800	
	Laererinde, h.g.	1150	1250						
	Laererinde, l.g.	900	975		1050	1150			
4. Fredrikstad	Laerer, h.g.	2100							
	Laerer, l.g.	1400	1550		1700	1850		2000	2100
	Laererinde, h.g.	1200							

[31] Reported in 1905 as already effective or to become effective immediately.

	Laererinde, l.g.	1000		1100			1200		
5. Drammen	Overlaerer	2600							
	Laerer, h.g.	2300		2400					
	Laerer, l.g.	1400	1600		1800	2000		2100	2300
	Laererinde, h.g.	1300		1400					
	Laererinde, l.g.	900	1000		1100	1200		1300	
6. Horten	Laerer, h.g.	2000		2200					
	Laerer, l.g.	1300	1500		1700	1850		2000	
	Laererinde, h.g.	1100		1200					
	Laererinde, l.g.	900	950		1000	1050		1100	
7. Tonsberg	Overlaerer	2500	2650		2800				
	Laerer, h.g.	2400	1600		1800	2000		2200	2400
	Laerer, l.g.	1400							
	Laererinde, h.g.	1300							
	Laererinde, l.g.	900	980		1060	1140		1220	1300
8. Kongsberg	Laerer, h.g.	1800							
	Laerer, l.g.	1300	1450		1600	1700		1800	
	Laererinde, h.g.	1100							
	Laererinde, l.g.	700	800		900	1000		1100	

CHAPTER III

COURSES OF STUDY IN STATE SCHOOLS

I. INTRODUCTORY—RISE, DEVELOPMENT, AND PRESENT FORM OF THE CURRICULUM

1. Origin and evolution of the course of study

We come now to a consideration of the course of study in the school system as it has evolved and is now operative. As was true throughout other parts of Europe, so in Norway, education during the middle ages issued almost exclusively from the cloister and cathedral schools (*Dom-og Kathedral Skoler*), and in them are found the germs of most modern courses of study. Inasmuch as the successive steps in the evolution of the recent schools of Europe from the earlier forms vary but little in the several countries, and since the subject is already familiar to nearly all students of education, we omit any technical discussion of that interesting feature of history, and refer the reader to any of the several works treating it fully. Suffice it to say, the aim of the church in maintaining these earlier schools centered in the development of a qualified clergy about whom should be gathered a loyal following, well-trained in the dogmas, doctrines, and traditions of the organization.

a. The early schools; their work, influence, and development in Norway

At this time the monk and a small company of disciples constituted the school. The little group studied together from day to day in and about the cloister or cathedral. Among them, very naturally, certain new thoughts and ideals sprung up. The masters saw the new developments if they were not themselves parties to them. As the newer thoughts became fixed in the youthful minds, individual interests pressed harder and harder still until provision was made for extending the work of instruction as well as for widening the scope of activities within the schools. While the aim was at first to give instruction and discipline in lines necessary to a clerical career, it changed by degrees until it included branches useful in legitimate occupations other than that of the clergy. However, the diversifying of school activities and the enrichment of the program of study did not keep pace with the changes that were taking place in other phases of the social cosmos. A spirit of unrest grew to proportions almost ungovernable until the middle age renaissance in learning removed the fetters and brought relief by effecting systems of education very fitting to the requirements. Great credit is due to the leaders in the Reformation for the part they played in placing means for instruction and education upon a more secure and permanent basis, and for the service they rendered in giving to the schools certain vitality that had rarely, if ever, been characteristic of any similar institution.

The new type of school bore a stamp of general approval which enabled it to gain a momentum which was not soon to be overcome. In fact, the schools of all the more civilized countries are still largely dominated by traditions dating back to the epoch-making works of such men as Erasmus, Luther, Melanchthon, and Sturm.

Now the ideas of these famous educators were less subjected to change in Norway than in the centers from whence they came. Until the union between this country and Denmark came to an end in 1814, very little thought was given to advancing educational interests in Norway. The work of her cathedral schools had been little improved during the centuries that had passed since their establishment. When at last Norway became a free constitutional state and these Norsemen breathed the air of freedom, felt the exhilaration of greater personal liberties, realized that their destiny was to be of their own making, and fully sensed their important responsibilities in the situation, they all, ecclesiasts and politicians, capitalists and laborers, combined in developing their schools in ways calculated to lift the masses to higher intellectual planes. The changes wrought were in relation to what was to be taught and to the extension of learning. An opportunity for instruction was given to every youth in the land.

For a long time the ancient languages formed the bulk of higher learning, while in the primary schools only the rudiments of a few subjects were attempted. Social tendencies soon required an increase in the number of branches to be taught, and also laid added weight upon the importance of such study as would be of benefit in vocational activities. Accordingly, mathematics, history, geography, and nature study became more prominent features in all schools. One of the best characteristics of the work throughout is that the mother-tongue has been at all times a dominating factor through every grade of their schools. Later in the process a demand for the modern foreign languages was responded to favorably and they took places in the curriculum of the higher school. These changes bring us down through the last century to the recent forms in courses of study and we shall introduce the reader immediately into the present situation.

2. Three sections of schools

Besides the institutions for higher learning there are now three distinct sections in the school system of Norway, viz.: Primary School, Middle School, and Gymnasium. The primary school is designed to provide education of an elementary type for every citizen of the country. By vital cooperation and the exercise of great care in organization, distribution, supervision, and inspection of these schools, the people have overcome illiteracy and have reduced truancy to a minimum—almost to a negligible factor. They are unitedly converted to the belief that an enlightened populace is a necessity to the continuity of desirable institutions, to the development of resources, and to the maintenance of worthy traditions. To secure for all the essentials of good and intelligent citizenship, an attempt has been made to have the curriculum for the primary schools include the branches of study which have meaning in every walk of life, and which enhance the efficiency of each citizen in his individual activities. In short, it is the intent that all the people shall have the more abundant life which comes with a thorough, general, elementary education; and, at the same time, that they shall be prepared for the higher schools which build on the broad foundation of the common school.

Following the primary schools are the middle schools which lead still farther in the pathway of intellectual development those whose situation in life enables them to proceed with school work. Besides carrying forward the lines of study begun in the lower school with added vigor and exactitude, they include a large amount of work in foreign modern languages. Thus we see that this second section in the great institution of learning fills in the elementary framework, enriches the fund of information, adds a considerable amount of culture, and paves the way for the more liberal training to follow in the next section.

The Gymnasium succeeds and builds directly upon the work of the middle school. Its function is to provide a liberal culture and education suited to the needs and desires of those who become in large part the leaders in all phases of political, professional, or other social careers.

Thus we note that the succeeding steps taken in the educational ladder are in harmony with and dependent upon preceding work. While only a correspondingly small number pass to the summit, all the people enjoy the advantages of the broad fundamentals and generalizations which lie at the base of their educational system and equip very well for the common walks and vocations of life. In our discussion we shall separate the work of the three sections and consider them one at a time. It seems advisable to handle them in this way, and we believe that a more adequate conception of the work as a whole will be obtained by offering first the part affecting all the people and dealing with the primary schools.

II. THE PRIMARY SCHOOLS

1. Rural and city

The primary schools are of two kinds,—those specially designed for the rural sections of the country and others provided for the towns and cities, the latter being somewhat richer in curricula, more complete in organization, and more thorough in operation than the former. Considering the fact that such uniformity characterizes the courses of study in the various schools, it will be necessary to present but one outline for each class of schools. An effort has been made to select courses that are representative and which clearly set forth typical conditions. Table VIII gives the program of work offered in one of the rural communes, and shows the number of hours per week devoted to each branch of study for the seven years in the course. Just after the legislative act of 1889, the Department sent out a "normal plan" which served as a guide in arranging the time-tables for rural municipalities. As a result great uniformity exists.

2. Schedules of courses

TABLE VIII

Table Showing the Number of Hours per Week for Each Branch of Instruction in the Course of Study in Fredrikvaern Commune.[32]

Year	I.	II.	III.	IV.	V.	VI.	VII.	Total
Religion	7	7	5	6	6	6	6	43
Norwegian	10	8	8	8	8	6	6	54
Mathematics	6	5	4	6	4	6	6	37
Geography			2	2	3	3	3	13
History			2	2	3	3	3	13
Nature Study	2	3	1	2	2	2	2	14
Writing	5	5	4	4	2	2	2	24
Drawing			1	2	2	2	2	9
Vocal Music		2	1	2	2	2	2	11
Manual Training			2	2	4	6	6	20
Gymnastics				2	2	2	2	8
Total	30	30	30	38	38	40	40	246

The program just above is normal and typical in every respect. The schools are very uniform in their work and, as previously stated, no further tables are necessary in order to give a concise idea of the work generally presented in the rural districts of the entire country.

The second program selected is the one used in the primary schools of Christiania.[33] The schools of this city are among the best and are taken as models for a number in other cities and towns.

The comparative table on page 48 clearly evidences the similarities already referred to and, at the same time, serves to indicate all variations. However, in the making of comparisons, difference in the number and distribution of hours is more a matter of method or correlation between branches than an indication of actual difference in accomplishment. For example, a large number of hours for writing *may* mean exclusively work in practice writing, but it is very probable that it will include a considerable amount of work in the mother-tongue or a definite correlation with nature study, history, or religion. The fundamental standard by which work is judged or measured is whether it prepares the pupil fully for work in the middle school.

[32] Year 1905.

[33] Year 1910-1911.

TABLE IX

Course of study showing weekly hours in Christiania Primary Schools.

DIVISION	FIRST						SECOND				THIRD					
YEAR[34]	I.		II.		III.		IV.		V.		VI.		VII.		Total	
SEX	B[35]	G[36]	B	G	B	G	B	G	B	G	B	G	B	G	B	G
Religion	6-2	6-2	6-2	6-2	6-2	6-2	4	3	4	3	4	4	3	3	24	22
Norwegian	12	11	10	8	8	7	5	5	5	4	5	4	5	5	50	44
Mathematics	5	4	4	4	4	3	4	3	3	3	3	3	3	3	26	23
Geography			3	2	2	2	1	1	1	1	1	1	1	1	9	8
History					2	2	2	2	1	1	1	1	2	2	8	8
Nature Study							1	1	2	2	2	2	2	2	7	7
Writing	4	4	4	3	3	2	2	2	1	1	1	1	1	1	16	14
Drawing							2		2	2	2	2	2	2	8	6
Vocal Music					1	1	1	1	1	1	1	1	1	1	5	5
Manual Training		2		4		4		4	2	4	2	4	2	4	6	26
Gymnastics					2-2	0	2	2	2	2	2	1	2		9	5
Total	24	24	24	24	24	24	24	24	24	24	24	24	24	24	168	168

[34] Year 1910-1911.
[35] *B* refers to boys, *G* to girls.
[36] *B* refers to boys, *G* to girls.

a. Comparisons

TABLE X

Comparative table of Courses of Study in ten cities.

	Religion		Norwegian		Mathematics		Geography		History		Nature Study		Writing		Drawing		Vocal Music		Manual Training		Gymnastics		Total	
City / Sex	B[37]	G[38]	B	G	B	G	B	G	B	G	B	G	B	G	B	G	B	G	B	G	B	G	B	G
Christiania	24	22	50	44	26	23	9	8	8	8	7	7	16	14	8	6	5	5	6	26	9	5	168	168
Bergen	21	21	55	53	29	28	8	8	9	9	8	7	10	8	9	8	5	5	8	24	10	7	172	178
Trondhjem	23	22	57	51	31	27	12	11	11	11	8	8	18	15	7	4	4	5	8	29	9	7	188	190
Stavanger	22	22	63	57	30	30	8	8	11	11	7	7	12	10	4	4	5	5	10	23	8	5	180	182
Drammen	24	24	52	47	29	25	8	8	8	8	6	5	17	13	5	3	5	5	6	25	8	5	168	168
Kristiansand	22	22	49	49	25	25	10	10	11	11	8	7	13	13	5	5	5	5	6	8	8	6	162	161
Aalesund	27	27	46	44	26	22	6	6	11	11	6	5	16	15	4	3	5	5	6	21	9	5	162	164
Fredrikshald	21	22	52	44	25	23	10	9	9	7	5	6	14	11	5	6	6	6	8	24	7	4	162	162
Skien	21	21	47	44	25	24	10	8	9	8	7	5	16	14	4	4	5	5	10	24	8	5	162	162
Kristiansund	24	24	50	47	27	26	8	8	9	8	8	7	18	15	3	3	5	5	6	20	10	5	168	168

[37] *B* refers to boys, *G* to girls.
[38] *B* refers to boys, *G* to girls.

b. Subjects emphasized

RELIGION, READING, RECKONING, RITING

The four R's in Norway's educational system form the center of their educational endeavors. Only a superficial glance at the tables presented is necessary in order to notice their prominence throughout the course of study. While the amount of time devoted to them is in itself a sufficiently strong indication of their predominance, we must also carry in mind an allowance for closest possible correlation between them as constant and additional factors along the same line. Bearing these things in mind we enter at once upon the discussion of the course of study or school plan. Though the programs presented and digest of plans following or accompanying are taken from particular schools, the discussion throughout will be general unless otherwise specified. For varied reasons, but chiefly because they are typical, specific, and concrete, the courses of study used in Christiania—primary and secondary—are chosen as illustrations. The following is not a verbatim translation of Christiania's plan of instruction but an abbreviated statement of the work as outlined in their published school plan (*Skoleplan*). I have endeavored to select the more vital points throughout and to represent them as exactly as a condensed version renders possible. Where inaccuracies or omissions occur they are due to a demand for economy—the things omitted not being regarded as absolute essentials to a correct representation of the intent and spirit of the work as carried on.

3. OUTLINE OF SUBJECTS OF INSTRUCTION

a. Religion

Aim. The aims of instruction in religion are to develop the religious instincts of the children and to instill in them a recognition of Christianity, out of which may grow a healthy Christian life and a clear conception of the church.

To attain these, an effort is made to impart the following fund of information:

Definite acquaintance with the more important parts of Bible history, with the chief events in church history, and with the catechism according to the Evangelical Lutheran creed.

First Division

Class I. (Six half hour periods weekly.) Instruction during the beginning weeks consists in simple stories, songs, hymns, prayers, and conversations designed to impart a knowledge of Christianity, ethics, and morals; to effect definite connections with previous home training; and to awaken and develop religious and moral attitudes in the children preparatory to the more direct instruction to follow.

The real instruction in Christianity or religion begins with Bible stories selected from the Old and New Testaments and specially adapted to the understanding of the children and their ability to master the same. The following stories are among the ones used: The Story of Joseph, Samuel and Hannah, David and Goliath, The Birth of Jesus, The Three Wise Men, Jesus in the Temple, Jesus Feeding the Five Thousand, Jesus Raising the Widow's Son, Jesus Blessing the Children,

Jesus Teaching the Disciples How to Pray. The stories are presented orally and explained and elucidated in such a way that the children may receive clear and vivid pictures of the persons and events referred to, appreciate their connections with the Holy Scriptures, and be able to rehearse the narratives in an intelligent manner. Whenever possible the religious or moral content of the conversation should be brought to a climax in a simple passage of Scripture, a response from the catechism, or a verse of some hymn, which should be memorized.

Class II. (Six half hour periods weekly.) Bible stories from Old and New Testaments taken mainly from the time of the patriarchs and Moses. Among them are the following:

From Old Testament: The Creation and Eden, The Fall, Cain and Abel, The Flood, The Call of Abraham, Abraham and Lot, The Birth and Offering of Isaac, The Marriage of Isaac, Esau and Jacob, Isaac Blessing His Sons, Jacob's Flight, The Birth and Rearing of Moses, The Call of Moses, Moses Before Pharaoh, The Exodus from Egypt.

From New Testament: The Birth of Jesus, Jesus' Entry into Jerusalem, Jesus Suffering in the Garden of Gethsemane, Jesus' Death on the Cross, The Burial of Jesus, The Resurrection of Jesus, The Outpouring of the Holy Ghost. Instruction is exclusively oral. Historical references are disregarded. Historical situations are frequently clarified by references to the history of civilization and geography. New phases of God's dealings with men and their attitudes toward Him are singled out and presented for consideration. Passages of Scripture and others from the catechism or hymns are treated in connection with the Bible stories as they are told.

Class III. (Six half hour periods weekly.) Biblical history up to and including the time of Solomon, characteristic stories from the prophetic period, and selections of Scripture from the New Testament designated officially for study in reference to certain church holidays. Among the topics included we find: The Tower of Babel, God's Covenant with Abraham, The Visit of the Three Men, The Lord Visits Sodom and Gomorrah, Jacob Serving Laban, Jacob's Return, The Travel to Sinai, The Giving of the Law, The Unfaithfulness of the People, The Travels from Sinai to Jordan, The Death of Moses, Joshua Leading the People into Canaan, Gideon, Ruth, Samuel, Saul Becomes King, Saul Rejected, God Chooses David to be King, David and Jonathan, Saul Pursuing David, The Death of Saul, David Chosen to be King by the People, The Fall and Restitution of David, Absalom, The Last Days of David's Life, Solomon, Elias, Jonah, Daniel. The matter covered in Classes I and II is again taken up, to which the above is added in historical connection. To this material Biblical geography and cultural history are added as needed, while hymns, passages of Scripture, or selections from the catechism are continually used. Through constant reviews the moral and religious contents from the various sources are connected into successive groups, each group centering around the life of some prominent Biblical character. Instruction is chiefly oral, though some reading from text is a privilege which may be indulged in as an aid. A certain amount of catechismal work may be assigned as home lessons.

Second Division

Class IV. (Boys four hours, girls three hours, weekly.) New Testament history centering in the stories of Jesus' childhood, His miracles, and His easier parables. New stories taken up: The Birth of John the Baptist Foretold, The Birth of Jesus Foretold, The Birth of John the Baptist, Jesus Presented in the Temple, The Flight into Egypt, Appearance of John the Baptist, The Baptism of Jesus, Jesus is Tempted, The First Disciples Come to Jesus, The Marriage in Cana, Jesus Visits Nazareth, Jesus Choosing the Twelve Apostles, Jesus Heals the Centurion's Servant, The Death of John the Baptist, Jesus Healing the Palsied, Jesus Raising Jairus' Daughter, The Woman of Canaan, Parable of the Unmerciful Servant, The Good Samaritan, Jesus at the House of Martha and Mary, Parables of the Lost Sheep and the Lost Coin, Parable of the Prodigal Son, Dives and Lazarus, Healing of the Ten Lepers, Parable of the Publican and Pharisee, Parable of the Marriage of the King's Son, Easter, Pentecost. The extent to which details of stories, Biblical geography, cultural history, and passages of Scripture or catechism are included is governed by the maturity and education of the children. In this class considerable attention is given to the reading of hymns and New Testament Scriptures from the four Gospels (elucidating obscure passages and difficult sentences), to connections between Bible stories and history, and to chronological sequence.

Class V. (Boys four hours, girls three hours, weekly.) Continued instruction in New Testament history, especially the parables of Jesus and the story of his passion and resurrection. To this is added the account of the founding of the first Christian church and its spread by the efforts of the chief apostles. The work includes the following new stories: Jesus and Nichodemus, Jesus and the Samaritan Woman, Jesus Commences to Speak in Parables, The Transfiguration of Jesus, Peter's Confession, The Man Born Blind, Jesus the Good Shepherd, The Raising of Lazarus, Jesus in the House of Zacchaeus, Jesus in Bethany, Parable of the Labourers in the Vineyard, Parable of the Ten Virgins, Washing of Feet, The Lord's Supper, Jesus in Gethsemane, Jesus Before the High Priest and the Sanhedrin, Jesus Before Pilate and Herod, Crucifixion of Jesus, Christ's Burial, The Resurrection, Jesus Appears to the Two Disciples on the Way to Emmaus, He Appears to the Disciples in Jerusalem, He Appears at the Sea of Tiberias, The Great Commission to the Disciples, His Ascension, The Outpouring of the Holy Ghost on Pentecost, The First Miracle and First Persecution, Stephen, The Ethiopian Eunuch, Saul, Cornelius, Paul Preaching the Gospel to the Gentiles.

Bible reading, the catechism, Bible history, and hymns are studied as in former classes, but more intensively. Besides the catechism, passages of Scripture, containing great Christian and moral truths are to be impressed and memorized verbatim. Continuous reviews through the years enable the children to connect several stories into groups, and to acquire complete information regarding the life and work of Christ. A small instruction book is used. First part and Article I of the second part are studied.

Third Division

Class VI. (Four hours weekly.) Bible history and Old Testament taken up simultaneously—Bible reading and ecclesiastical history alternating. A deeper knowledge of sacred history is sought. Striking illustrations of God's plan of salvation operating among the Jews are given, designed to enable the children to appreciate the redemptive meaning of Old Testament history. Emphasis is placed on the period just preceding the time of Christ. New stories introduced: The Division of the Kingdom, Elisha, The Downfall of the Kingdom of Israel, Isaiah, Jeremiah, The Fall of the Kingdom of Judah, The Jews under Babylonian Captivity, Their Return from Captivity, The Last Four Hundred Years.

Familiarity with Old Testament Scriptures and history, Biblical geography, and cultural history is to be gained. Articles II and III of the second part, and the third, fourth, and fifth parts of the instruction book are taken up.

Class VII. (Three hours weekly.) One Gospel—Matthew—is read connectedly and followed by a treatment of selected parts from the Acts of the Apostles in connection with the work of Biblical history in the fourth and fifth grades. All materials previously gathered from the various sources are again taken up, applied, and centered.

Narratives relating to important periods of the church. Among them:—The Persecutions (under Nero, Polycarpus), The Victory of Christianity (Constantine), The Christian Ceremonies, Augustine, Hermits and Monks, The Spread of Christianity, The Popes, The Crusades, The Preparation for the Reformation, The Lutheran Reformation (Luther, the Jesuits, the Catholic Mission), The Lutheran Church in the Seventeenth and Eighteenth Centuries, in the Eighteenth and Nineteenth Centuries, The Mission, Bible Societies.

The aim in this division is to give information regarding the development of the church in general, and of the Lutheran church in particular. Narratives are grouped around great central characters—Christian personages. A realization of the lofty aims of Christianity on the part of the children together with an appreciation of their duties and responsibilities as members of the Christian church is the intent. By means of an instruction book the main divisions of church history, general history, and the history of Norway are correlated. Information contained in the hymn book acquaints the children with the ceremonial order of the ecclesiastical year as well as with the contents and order of the book itself. The study of previously memorized hymns and verses is emphasized and enlarged upon.

It is to be remembered that in Norway church and state are united. Religious and scholastic interests are under the direction of the Department of Ecclesiastical and Educational affairs. The minister of this department of State is one of the King's cabinet. Here we find one of the numerous attempts at the solution of the vexing question of moral instruction, or, to be more exact, religious instruction in the public schools. While the provisions for this teaching are not faultless, and though their course of instruction could not be adopted for use in America with its medley of religious prejudices, yet we must acknowledge that they are well adapted to the needs and desires of the people served. The citizenship of the country is homogenous religiously, almost universally Lutheran, and their traditions militate against any change in religious creed. The teaching of religion in the schools has been the practice for generations, the instruction is taken as a matter of course, and it exerts its beneficient influences upon all.

There are a number of important features of this moral instruction which press their claims for special mention, but we cannot discuss them all. A few, however, demand some attention. The statement of the proverb, that as the twig is bent so will the tree be inclined, has been borne out in practice times without number. Here, it seems to me, is one more illustration. Throughout their whole school life—that receptive, appropriating, formative period—the children have constantly before them ideals that are elevating, examples that are inspiring, and admonitions that tend to create and develop within them an ambition to excel in beauty of character. That the morals of society are not kept more nearly pure by this procedure seems a psychological impossibility. Again a rather successful attempt is made to have the home and school cooperate along the lines of personal purity. In fact the home, the school, and the church join hands and supplement each other in all efforts in religious and moral training. True it is that striking examples of nobility of character, high ideals, and moral worth abound in profane history as well as in sacred, in secular life as well as in religious, in living characters as truly as in those of past ages, but the school system of Norway provides ample opportunity for presenting all of these things in connection with their regular instruction in the various subjects taught, and, in addition, furnishes particularized instruction which makes a specialty of moral and religious development. It seems imperative that, when these ennobling lessons are thus vividly presented, the powers of imitation and habit should combine in the creation of stronger and nobler characters.

Nevertheless, when religious instruction is made a requirement, it too frequently becomes formal and literal rather than spiritual and lifegiving. That this great misfortune is the case in some of the secondary schools of Norway is an indictment which cannot be denied. However, in the primary schools the instruction is fruitful and important. As a consequence of these conditions the statement is common among many that in looking back over the years of religious instruction they recall numerous happy instances of earnest, heartfelt prayer and Bible stories accompanied by intense feeling on the part of the teacher. Other experiences reveal the fact that some of the teaching profession had not the sincerity and feeling back of their instruction required in order to give vitality and meaning to the lessons presented.

The entire question of instruction in morals in our public schools is one of pressing importance. It is being agitated in many lands today and a solution is sorely needed. Were all classes of society united as to what should be included in this instruction the matter would adjust itself very readily. However, social conditions in a single nation are more or less diverse, and between different nations still greater breaks are to be found. In fact the ideals and conceptions of society are so varied that no one present system would suffice for all. Could a code of ethics be formulated which would meet universal approval then its adoption and use might be hoped for. Until then each nation must necessarily follow the plan which seems best adapted to its social requirements. As already stated, the people of Norway are nearly all adherents to the Lutheran creed so there are very few dissenters from the common rule. Provision is made in the law that those who do not adhere to the state church and object to receiving instruction in this particular line may, upon request of parent or guardian, be excused from such instruction.[39]

b. Norwegian

Aim. It is the aim of the instruction in Norwegian to further the mental development of children, especially their linguistic ability. In this course of activity they should acquire:

(1) Efficiency in apprehending and assimilating what they hear or read, confident readiness in reading, plain articulation, and correct and natural accentuation.

(2) Efficiency in expressing themselves orally and in writing without making any serious errors in the common usage of language or the rules of composition.

(3) Efficiency in the use of the grammar of the mother-tongue which is necessary for the above measure of attainments.

First Division

Class I. (Boys twelve hours, girls eleven hours, weekly.) A suitable number (twelve or fifteen) of interesting children's stories are told and utilized for the special purposes of widening the circle of the children's imagination and developing in them ability in observation, conception, and expression. An effort is made to render the general contents of the stories lucid through explanations, while the features arousing special interest in the minds of the pupils are made the objects of more detailed conversation. An effort is made to train the children in correct, free, and easy expression in connected sentences, and to develop in them the ability to rehearse their stories freely and connectedly.

Reading. The aim is ability to read the primer (*ABC-en*) with assurance and in a clear tone, properly articulating and accenting each word and syllable.

Written exercises. The object of the written work is to teach the children to write words and simple sentences which have just been read orally or have been seen in the primer or on the blackboard.

Class II. (Boys ten hours, girls eight hours, weekly.) Twenty or thirty of the most interesting and valuable selections (prose and poetry) contained in the reader are made the objects of special and thorough treatment. Comments, questions, elucidating explanations, and conversations are means employed in securing a vivid appreciation of the contents and in developing ability in their easy rehearsal. The other pieces are treated in a more cursory manner, only the larger views and the more general understanding of them being attempted.

Special attention is given to having all readings slow with loud, plain, and correct articulation and proper accentuation. Habitual mistakes are carefully eliminated. Story telling is also a feature of the year's work.

Written exercises, made up of sentences and short parts of readings, conversations, or stories are given frequently and for short periods. Here the names of

[39] Law for City Schools, Sec. 4.

letters and spelling are attended to with great care.

Class III. (Boys eight hours, girls seven hours, weekly.) Twenty or thirty paragraphs from the reader are given special attention—the remainder cursory. The plan of work is about the same as for Class II. Considerable attention is given to the rehearsing of the reading lesson by the pupils. Some reproductions are to be quite detailed and exact though they are not to be given in the exact words of the text. Still other selections receive more general treatment. A few of the most pleasing poems should be memorized. Greater readiness in slow and even reading with loud and clear expression and proper natural accentuation should be sought.

Written exercises. Selections from the language work giving special and rather extended attention to spelling, punctuation, and grammatical constructions and forms. The teacher sets examples of correct punctuation, etc.

Second Division

Class IV. (Five hours weekly.) A select number (20-30) of pieces from the reader treated as in the former classes, though more exhaustively; and, in addition, quite a wide range of selections chosen for more cursory reading. A considerable amount of information regarding the topics treated and explanations of literary expressions should form important parts of the instruction in this class. Here, as in both preceding and succeeding classes, it should be the aim to have the children make their meanings plain when conversing upon the selections read, at least to the degree of their ability and development. Parts of former conversations on various topics should also be recalled and woven into their discussions.

Written exercises. These shall include features previously studied, and introduce more detailed and finer discriminations in grammatical usages and forms.

Class V. (Boys four hours, girls five hours, weekly.) Exhaustive study of a few selections and cursory reading in large quantities as before. Careful and abundant training in oral expression. Specific and detailed rehearsal of topics discussed in which an increasing amount of knowledge gained through study, experience, and thought is utilized. Short stories are read. Poems are memorized. Progress in clear and distinct articulation and easy and natural emphasis in harmony with refined speech is continuously a requirement.

Written exercises. A continuation of former exercises and a considerable amount of copying, or the writing of abstracts of lesson content, especially during the second half year. Orthographic, grammatical, and rhetorical forms are entered into more exhaustively and their niceties urged. Through continued practice in preparing and writing compositions, extra work in copying, and special study of orthography and punctuation, the children, by the close of this their fifth year of schooling, should be quite capable in punctuation as well as spelling, though they should not be expected to spell and punctuate independently with accuracy.

Third Division

Class VI. (Boys five hours, girls six hours, weekly.) Reading from a selected portion of the reader. Conversations, information, explanations, and linguistic elucidations are to be entered into according to necessity. Increasing stress is here laid on the work of drawing out the thoughts, ideas, and knowledge of the pupils, and of inciting them to more independent, intellectual effort.

Written exercises. Continued as previously though introducing larger amounts of independently selected forms of expression and insisting on greater accuracy in punctuation. Letter writing is added.

Class VII. (Five hours weekly.) Selections from the reader and supplementary reading from recommended books calculated to awaken, develop, and educate. Special attention given to the most important authors.

Written exercises. Compositions on topics of interest, letter writing, business correspondence including applications, invoices, advertisements, and telegrams.

The methods employed in presenting the mother-tongue are quite plainly set forth in the foregoing outline. Though the content is not so specifically defined, the general lines are indicated in such a way as to give very adequate insight thereinto. Some of the methods of presentation seem somewhat cumbersome and rather antiquated. This impression is due chiefly to terminology. The actual work in the schoolrooms is flexible, free, and, as a rule, attractive. The latitude granted to the teachers in all their work admits of almost unlimited individual initiative. Many of their teachers are quite expert in the most modern methods.

The utilitarian idea which pervades every phase of their school work is especially noticeable in the teaching of their own language. In harmony with this idea, let me call attention to the fact that, from the first, constant use is made of every attainment in both oral and written form. The oral work embraces the reading of the text, reading from the blackboard, and conversational exercises on the special topics being considered. Written work on the same lessons include copying of certain selections or parts of them and original expressions in regard to the contents of lessons read. In the advanced grades these written exercises become more and more extended and complicated until they amount to complete essays. Special attention is given to correct forms of expression and to the acquirement of habits of clear and distinct enunciation. The child, who from his earliest school days becomes habituated to exact pronunciations, is very liable—almost sure—to spell correctly; and, when constant use is made of the language in written exercises, the accepted and approved forms of expression become the fixed usages.

Now their treatment of the mother-tongue is a combination of our reading, spelling, language lessons, grammar, rhetoric, and literature, all taught in their natural order as they arise through actual use. Incidentally, vast amounts of biography, history, geography, and natural science as well as writing are included. The richness of content and thoroughness of treatment deserve careful consideration in the writing of courses and still more in their application. Specialization in phases of a single subject in lower schools nearly always means waste of energy, scattering of forces, and disappointment in the end. On the contrary, unification and close correlation result in economy of time and effort, and issue in more worthy attainments. The several fields of thought are already too much isolated from each other, and unless some guards are erected the individual fields also will be broken up and their distinctive phases so divorced from one another that their cooperative tendencies and values will become void and their relationships will be lost sight of. Norwegian is easily the preponderant study in Norway's schools, but, since it is so inclusive, it probably deserves the large amount of time devoted to it.

The long lists of supplementary readings now provided in our American schools exert a wholesome influence. Their constant revision and extension furnish materials which in the hands of skilled teachers, guarantee to the pupils sure knowledge and ability in the use of the mother-tongue. The limitless resources in English literature, America's lavish provision for higher education and professional training, and the freedom granted to our teaching profession leave the teachers of our language without excuse. The pupils studying English in America have a right to expect the best. One condition which frequently militates against first class work in this line is that school boards all too frequently fail to realize that being a teacher of English means more than merely hearing lessons so many times a week. A very large part of the most important work must be done aside from class exercises. If there be any teacher justified in asking a reduction in hours of instruction it is the teacher of the mother-tongue.

c. Mathematics

Aim. Readiness in the four mathematical operations in whole numbers, decimal numbers, and simple fractions, written and oral. Ability to independently solve various examples in the forms in which they generally appear in practical life, also examples in proportion and examples in percentage, together with problems of planes and solids. Course and mode of its execution as given in a text—Instruction in Mathematics (*Regneundervisningen*)—followed in all essentials.

First Division

Class I. (Boys five hours, girls four hours, weekly.) Through constant use of illustrative material (objects about the room, wooden pins, cubes, the children's fingers, etc.) the children are taught to gradually become acquainted with the numbers to ten, twenty, thirty, and on up to one hundred; and they are afforded continuous practice in reading, writing, and explaining the numbers, as well as in performing simple solutions in the four arithmetical operations. At the close of the year the children should be able to count to one hundred forward and backward. They must know how to manipulate the numbers from one to ten in adding to or subtracting from any number less than one hundred, and be able, by the assistance of the tables, to answer questions in multiplication (two's to five's). and some questions in division. Chief importance attaches to the ability of the children to use the numbers from one to thirty.

Class II. (Four hours weekly.) Acquaintance with and ability to read and write any number up to one million.

Mental arithmetic. Continuation of operations begun in Class I. When proficient in adding and subtracting units to and from one hundred, tens and units are taken up in the same way. Examples in easy multiplication, with occasional use of division, carried on throughout the year.

Tablet work. Addition and subtraction of numbers up to one million. In the operations coin, measure, and weight denominations are used, and are illustrated by coins, measures, and weights.

Class III. (Boys four hours, girls three hours, weekly.) Acquaintance with the numeral system up to and including millions. Continuous practice in reading, writing, and using numbers.

Mental operations. Addition and subtraction of numbers up to one hundred continued. Thereafter extend the numbers as far as the children can use them with certainty and rapidity. Multiplication of numbers up to one hundred by units.

Tablet work. More work in addition and subtraction going farther than to numbers with six ciphers. Multiplication of numbers with many ciphers by multipliers having one or more ciphers.

Second Division

Class IV. (Boys four hours, girls three hours, weekly.) Division with divisors having one or more ciphers. Separation of numbers into their individual factors. Finding of the least common multiple. After this a thorough drill in the four arithmetical operations with whole numbers—old and new exercises.

Mental and tablet exercises in closest relation to each other. In all mental operations, here or later, rapid and positive use should be made of the easier examples before the harder ones are fumbled or handled with uncertainty.

Class V. (Two hours weekly.) After the necessary preparation, practice in the three operations with decimal numbers. In connection with the consideration of plane surfaces the children should be given practice in measuring parallelograms, triangles, irregular quadrangles and many-sided surfaces—triangles should predominate.

Mental and tablet exercises parallel each other and are in intimate relation.

Third Division

Class VI. (Three hours weekly.) Preparatory practice in common fractions together with addition and subtraction of fractions having a common denominator and others which can easily be reduced to a common denominator. Multiplication and division using or including fractions. Further development with mental operations growing out of and in connection with tablet work.

Class VII. (Three hours weekly.) Percentage including interest, rebate, and discount. The calculating of cubes, prisms, pyramids, circles, cylinders, cones; also shortened pyramids, cones, and cylinders.

After this a general review so far as time admits.

Simple arithmetical operations occupy the entire field during the earlier years. The elementary algebraic forms and methods of solution are introduced relatively early, and minor geometric relations and operations are presented during the last (seventh) year of the lower schools. These latter features are radically different from our general procedure in the United States. We are in the habit of presenting the various mathematical subjects one at a time, completing one before another is considered to any extent whatever. For example, arithmetic is taken up and gone through, while parts of geometry and algebra which would be great aids in some of the arithmetical solutions are studiously avoided or excluded until the formal study of that particular subject is finally begun. The people of Norway, on the contrary, enter the larger field of mathematics and, in a more rational manner—a more psychological way—utilize available processes and forms at every opportunity. The phases of mathematics are not specialized into isolation but coordinated into a working unity. Instead of studying one subject throughout its intricacies and side issues before admitting consideration of other phases of mathematics, they make it the rule to utilize the elemental factors of the various mathematical subjects in every way possible. They give recognition to the simpler and more fundamental principles and operations regardless of the special phase of the subject to which they belong, and use the entire product as groundwork for succeeding steps in the science. In this way parts of algebra and geometry become valuable contributing preliminaries to higher arithmetical operations.

The texts used by the pupils are little more than a series of exercises. All teaching is done by the teacher and the texts are arranged in such a way that the children may have opportunity to become skilled in the principles evolved in class through application of them in the long lists of problems in their texts. Very little blackboard is provided for the pupils' use, hence but little blackboard work is accomplished. Each room has a small board on which the teacher of a pupil may go through solutions. Never have I seen more than one at a time working at the blackboard. While the limited use of blackboards generally calls for an increased amount of dependence upon intellectual activity and consequent increase in mental alertness, the free use of blackboards relieves the mind of unnecessary burdens which may as well be borne by crayon, and thus provides for the higher centers a freer activity in pushing on the quest for the unknown.

d. Geography

Aim. To obtain (1) A somewhat complete acquaintance with the fatherland; its conditions, commerce, manner of life. (2) Acquaintance with the geography of Europe, especially the countries to the north and the other longer civilized countries. (3) A view of the different continents and a closer acquaintance with lands and places which are of greatest importance to the fatherland. (4) Knowledge of the most important features of physical and mathematical geography.

First Division

Class II. (Boys three hours, girls two hours, weekly.) With continuous reference to local geography and places known to the children, the pupils are brought to understand geographical forms and relations in general. Special attention is given to charts and maps. Instruction begins with drawings (on blackboard and tablets) of the schoolroom; then extends to schoolgrounds, to the immediate surroundings with streets and some of the more important buildings; and then to the entire city with its environs, etc., etc. The children should become acquainted with the more important features of topography, soil, valleys, plains, ridges, mountains, seas, fjords, rivers, brooks, seasons, day and night, rising and setting of planets (sun, moon, and stars), flora and fauna, altitude, sea level, etc. From familiarity with the city and its surroundings the work extends to the entire fatherland which is considered in an elementary fashion. Herein are included elementary studies of coast line, principal systems of valleys, and location and size of cities.

Map drawing of small localities.

Class III. (Two hours weekly.) The map of Europe. Beginning with the fatherland, including its location with reference to other lands and seas as well as its relations thereto, enter into a study of other European countries in the order in which they would naturally be entered if touring from the fatherland. Subdivisions of the sea and land, also cities, railways, canals, rivers, and mountains are to be studied. Pictures are to be used in illustration. By the use of globes and other illustrative material, the discussion may be extended to other parts of the world. Each of the several divisions of the earth is to be treated in an elementary manner. Everything is to be outlined or indicated on the maps and charts—first by the teacher and later by the pupils.

Second Division

Class IV. (One hour weekly.) On the foundation of what was done in Class III the work shall be extended to the outlying divisions of Europe—Norway, Sweden, Denmark, The British Isles, France, Spain, Portugal, Italy, Russia. The study of maps is emphasized both for review and new work. Every land is considered with reference to the fatherland, other known lands, the equator, and the poles. Attention confined to typical aspects: description of a typical city, a manufacturing center, etc., special variations in climate, flora and fauna, chief natural scenery, commercial activities, products and conditions of the citizens. Readings on geographical topics are correlated with picture illustrations. Details and illustrations utilized as in Class III.

Class V. (One hour weekly.) Holland, Belgium, Germany, Switzerland, Austria, Hungary, and the Balkan peninsula are considered after the plan used in Class IV. After these European countries, foreign countries are discussed. Study and instruction in this class is in accord with the outlines of work in previous classes though more exhaustive and minute. India, China, the large islands in the Pacific Ocean, North Africa with its Sahara, Central Africa, The United States of America, Australia, etc., are also considered.

Third Division

Class VI. (One hour weekly.) The geography of the fatherland is gone through thoroughly with the aim of imparting to the children a rather complete knowledge of their country's nature, commerce, and life in its various localities. The chief points considered are: coast line, surface, water channels, climate—east and west—boundaries, inhabitants, life of the people, political divisions. This is to be constantly correlated with what has been learned previously of other European countries. Map drawing in detail. Review of former work.

Class VII. (One hour weekly.) The more important features of mathematical and physical geography are presented, being continuously illustrated by charts, maps, globes, astronomical plates, etc. The horizon, earth formations, zones, yearly and daily rotations, geographical breadth and length; the moon, its phases; the planets, etc., are important topics for study. Others are positions of continents and oceans with reference to each other, climate and physical features of the earth, the air, winds, changes in temperature, movements of the sea, the more important ocean streams (Gulf and Polar streams), etc. Throughout the study constant connections should be made between what is known in geography, natural history, and nature study.

The outline indicates both thoroughness and a close correlation with related fields of work. Beginning with the well-known in geography they gradually widen their horizon and establish connections with the more remote parts of the earth until the children obtain a moderately accurate appreciation and knowledge of this branch of study and get a view of its intricate relations with life and human activity. While the work of the course is generally characterized by thoroughness, their study of localities outside of Europe is simply a skimming over or a skipping glance.

To be sure time is insufficient to enable them to exhaust all opportunities; but, it would seem more consistent with their general idea of concentrating on matters which directly concern the fatherland and its subjects, did they bring the young into a more intimate acquaintance with America and a fuller appreciation of what America really means to Norway and Norwegians. Very few Norsemen are without vital interests here. Nearly all, it seems, have immediate relatives or very dear friends who have migrated from the native land and have established homes in the United States. It appears that it would be important for them to follow the path of their migrating brethren and acquaint themselves more fully with the geography of America. Its life, topography, commerce, and other distinctive features would add to their geography a chapter of unsurpassed values.

The work which is done is commendable for many reasons. The many-sided views obtained by varied methods of attack are rich and meaningful. Every pupil is ready with a full discussion in response to a question relating to their own country. Furthermore, they are informed with reference to the relationships existing between each country studied and the fatherland. These have been clearly pointed out. The perspective obtained through the study of physical and mathematical geography affords richer meaning to every day of life as well as to all the phenomena of nature.

e. History

Aim. The chief aim of instruction in history is to inspire the children's historic instincts and love for their country and people. In an effort to obtain this the following information is imparted: (1) A somewhat connected knowledge of the history of the fatherland together with the fundamental tendencies of the social order. (2) Acquaintance with the most significant incidents in general history.

First Division

Class III. (Two hours weekly.) Selected narratives from the history of the fatherland. The collection of stories includes the following: Harald the Fair Haired, Haakon the Good, Haakon Jarl, Olaf Trygveson, Olaf the Holy, Sverre Sigurdson, Haaken the Aged, Margaret and Albert, Christian the Second, Christian the Fourth, Tordenskjold, The Years 1807-1814, The Time of Pirates, Kristian August, Norway in 1814, Kristian Fredrik, Eidsvold, 17th of May, Norway's decennial celebration.

The stories are presented orally and are so detailed that the children get clear pictures of persons and incidents. The material of instruction is centered about particular and important persons and incidents in order to give them greater fixity. The pupils rehearse the stories they have been taught. Historic poems and songs of the fatherland which refer especially to people or incidents are studied in connection with the history. The material received through instruction in geography during the former year is utilized as groundwork in building up and enriching the historical ideas of the fatherland. The more important phases of social institutions are presented in a way suited to the capacity of the pupils. As the stories proceed, an attempt is made to awaken a degree of appreciation of their historical sequence.

Second Division

Class IV. (Two hours weekly.) Stories and descriptions regarding general history centering about the following points or topics: Ancient world kingdoms, Greeks, Romans, Germans, Norse, Papacy, great discoveries and inventions. Treatment here is similar to that given in Class III. Stories, anecdotes and pictures add life to regular routine. Stories of the fatherland are presented in very brief form and are given in order to effect connection with general events in world history. Here again geography is made the groundwork of history.

Class V. (One hour weekly.) Work carried on as previously. Narratives of events chiefly during the time from the Reformation to the French Revolution.

Central features studied: Luther and the time of the Reformation (Luther's childhood and youth, Karl V., extension of the Reformation, and the Thirty Years' War), the period of absolute monarchy, the time preceding the Revolution, science and discovery. Presentation of topics the same as previously given. Here is included also a considerable amount of culture history, descriptions from which are given in such a way that life among the higher classes, as well as among the oppressed, may be presented and appreciated.

Third Division

Class VI. (One hour weekly.) Work continued as heretofore. Stories from the time of the Revolution down to modern times. Among the materials used are the following topics: time of the Revolution, 1789-1800; Napoleon, 1800-1815; July and February Revolutions, Napoleon III., Germany's consolidation, discoveries and inventions, delineations of the history of civilization, and the advance of modern times in industries and means for communication.

Class VII. (Two hours weekly.) The history of the fatherland gone through in great detail and in a definitely connected manner. All work based upon what has been learned in former classes. The following are among the more important points considered: Norway in ancient times, Norway organized into a Christian kingdom, Norway's time of prosperity, Norway under internal wars, Norway under later kings of Swedish family and descent, Norway in union with Sweden and Denmark, Norway united to Denmark until 1661, time of absolute monarchy (1661-1814), Norway in 1814, Norway since 1814. In addition, the chief features of social institutions, the condition of the state, rights and obligations of citizens, state administration, communal affairs, and similar topics are discussed at some length.

By the assistance of a suitable text the presentation should impart to the pupils a moderately connected knowledge of the historical development of the fatherland up to the present time. The children should obtain clear insight into the inner historic situations; persons, events, and specific dates standing as contributors in the background. Historic sagas and related selections are used in connection. While attention centers in the history of the fatherland, important contemporary events in general history are kept constantly before the eyes, frequent reference being made to the studies in Classes IV-VI.

The stated aims, enumerated means, and outlined methods of presentation afford a fairly good idea of the work done in the study of history throughout the primary schools. It has been observed, perhaps by many, that instruction in history has been preceded by one year's study of geography, that the geography of the several countries precedes the history of the peoples inhabiting them, and that geographical appreciation is utilized as a foundation for instruction in history.

The main purposes of instruction in history are: development of patriotic and loyal citizens, intellectual training, and cultural information. The prized traits of citizenship are read, sung, and drilled into the daily life of every child in the entire country, and these impressions are fixed so definitely that they live through generations, even when the subjects are transplanted to foreign soils.

Story telling in the beginnings of history instruction affords an immediate appeal both to the children's interest in personal activities and to their liking for that form of instruction. The characters whose biographies are delineated are the men around whom national activities have centered. The bits of history related are of epoch-making incidents from the earliest times down to the present. Being presented through biography they have a personal touch and flavor which secure vital and immediate responses from the children.

There are still other features worthy of consideration. Incidents of historic interest are not only pointed out and studied but the scenes of these are actually visited. Here again we see the definite way in which history and geography are correlated. Too, since Norway has been favored by the gift of many literary geniuses, most historic characters and events have found place in literary classics. All along the way, songs, poems, and dramas having relation to national history are brought into the instruction in a living, real way. The children are given abundant opportunity to attain proficiency in relating historic events with information gained from the fields of geography, language, and literature.

f. Nature Study

Aim. Instruction in nature study attempts to awaken the children's interest in and regard for nature in all its expressions, and to exercise their thought powers and judgment so as to enable them to find or make connections between cause and effect. In order that their attention be centered upon the suitability to purpose, conformity to law, harmony and beauty, the children should have their thought directed to nature's creation and maintenance. Finally, the children through this instruction should obtain a conception of how mankind attempts to control nature and to utilize its strength in the promotion of human welfare.

Materials for instruction. Our bodily structure in the large or whole, as necessary to an understanding of the general conditions in man's physical life and as fundamental to instruction in health. The more important native and foreign animals and plants; their growth and life, together with their importance in nature's economy. The natural forces which have greatest significance for organic life and for man's efficiency.

Methods of instruction. Natural objects or representations of them in model or drawing, and operations of natural forces illustrated by experiments observed and written up. The accuracy of observations are tested by the pupil's oral or written accounts of what they see. Conditions and things familiar to the children in common life are the ones to be used above all others.

Class IV. (One hour weekly.) Short synopsis over our bodily structure (four hours). Present by oral instruction and through illustrative materials the skeleton, muscles, digestive organs, skin, circulation, respiratory organs. The same points may also be studied as they appear in the lower animals.

Mammals. (Twenty hours.) Horse, ass, cow, sheep, goat, reindeer, deer, elk, camel, cat, wild-cat, lion, tiger, dog, wolf, fox, marten, bear, swine, elephant, seal, whale, hare, rabbit, squirrel, rat, beaver, anteater, bat, monkey.

Fowls. (Ten hours.) Tame chickens, woodcock, sparrow, yellow hammer, bullfinch, lark, swallow, starling, dove, cuckoo, parrot, hawk, falcon, eagle, owl, heron, stork, duck, goose, swan, gull, ostrich, and others.

Instruction begins with typical animal forms which are illustrated by charts or drawings when the stuffed or mounted specimens are not at hand. The children are required to depend upon themselves as much as possible in finding out individual characteristics in the bodily structures of the chosen forms. Then bodily structure and habits are related, as are also their homes, food, color, and environment. Finally, the animal's meaning in the economy of nature and its value to man are the points studied. Along with the careful study of a typical form, related animals are examined in a more general and cursory manner. The children are taught to remember that while they have dominion over the animals they are at the same time under obligations to them. Disregard of these duties is looked upon as rudeness. Animal stories form a part of the instruction. After studying the chosen types a review takes notice of common characters and separates animals into classes. Instruction is based on a text.

Class V. (Two hours weekly.) *Plants.* (Forty hours.) *Dicotyledonous plants.* Bluebells, buttercups, strawberry, apple trees, pea, clover, beans, cherry, plum, dandelion, blueberry, heather, potato, tobacco, willow, birch, hazel, and others, studied under their regular headings or in their special families.

Monocotyledonous plants. Rye, barley, wheat, oats, timothy, lily of the valley, pine, fir, juniper, in connection with respective families.

Flowerless plants. Ferns, moss, mushrooms.

Foreign useful plants. Coffee, tea, cotton, sugar cane, rice, maize, orange, palms, spices. All plants are studied carefully under their respective subdivisions. As in the consideration of animals, the growth, vital organs, habitat, and use of plants are studied, as are also their grouping, fruit, etc. About fifty plants are studied carefully and others are related to them. The children are taught not to injure plants or trees.

Animals. (Twenty hours.) Adder, lizard, crocodile, turtle, frog, toad, mackerel, pike, salmon, trout, herring, haddock, flounder, eel, shark, cabbage butterfly, silk worm, moth, bee, bumble-bee, wasp, ant, fly, gnat, grasshopper, spider, lobster, crab, angleworm, leech, trichina, snail, mussel, star-fish, sea urchin, coral, sponge, etc. Instruction along same line as in Class IV.

Physics. (Sixteen hours.) Based on a text. Instruction to be accompanied by experiments whenever possible—otherwise illustrated by drawings and models.

Solids. Resistance to change in form: hardness, elasticity. Resistance to change of extensity: compressibility, porosity, adhesion, cohesion.

Liquids. No fixed form, apparent unchangeability of extensity, adhesion to solids, solution of solids, mixing of liquids, endosmose.

Gases. No definite form, attraction, diffusion, absorption.

Gravitation. Weight, units of weight, weighing, relation between weight and size, force of weight as a cause of movement, hindrances to movement, forces in equilibrium.

The lever. Balance, hand presses, on the principle of the lever.

Class VI. (Two hours weekly.) *Liquids.* (Eight hours.) Distribution of pressure, Archimedes' law, specific gravity, communicating shaft.

Properties of air. (Eight hours.) Archimedes' law, the atmosphere and its pressure, barometer, pumps and lifters, Mariotte's law.

Heat. (Twelve hours.) Different temperatures, effects of heat, expansion of bodies, the thermometer, maximum density of water, melting and freezing, evaporation and condensation, boiling, degree of pressure at the boiling point.

Transmission of heat by radiation and by conduction, good and poor conductors, temperature and humidity of the air, downward pressure, circulation of water, atmospheric currents, sources of heat, heat as force, steam pressure.

Sound. (Eight hours.) Origin of sound, its transmission, rate of transmission, the ear, tones, reflection of sound.

Light. (Ten hours.) Self-illuminating and dark bodies, transparent and opaque, straight path of light, shade, rate of transmission, reflection, refraction, diffusion of color, convex and concave lenses, microscope, telescope, camera, the eye, spectacles.

Magnetism. (Five hours.) The magnet and its poles, their reciprocal relations, magnetizing, difference magnetically in iron and steel, horseshoe magnet, compass.

Electricity. (Fifteen hours.) Electricity of friction, two kinds of electrical condition, conductors and insulators, communicating and distributing, electrical machines, lightning and thunder, lightning rods, electrical current, battery, electric light, electro-magnetism, telegraph, telephone, electricity which generates power.

Equilibrium and Motion. (Ten hours.) Motion with uniform, increasing, or decreasing rapidity; combination of motion and force (the parallelogram of power, center of gravity, the three conditions of balance, the beam, the inclined plane); work and vital force; experiment with the pendulum.

Class VII. (Two hours weekly.) *Physics.* (Sixteen hours.) Machines, block, tackle, windlass, the curved pivot, various driving forces (water wheel, steam engines, dynamos), application of machinery in the industries, railways and steamboats.

Chemistry. (Sixteen hours.) Ingredients of water and air, coal, carbonic acid, burning and oxidation. Fundamental elements as material in all bodies. Examples of elements: oxygen, hydrogen, nitrogen, carbon, chlorine, sulphur, phosphorus, aluminum, iron, silver, and gold. Examples for combinations: water, ammonia, sulphuric acid, rust, soda, cooking salt, lime, chalk, clay, quartz, ores. Examples of organic matter: starch, sugar, albumen, alchohol, fats. Instruction in chemistry consists in illustrations and descriptions of materials and experiments.

Structure and life of the human body. Study of health. (Thirty hours.) Based on text. Study of skeleton, muscles, nervous system, work and rest, sense organs and their use, digestive organs and processes, use of teeth, blood and circulation, breathing pure and impure air, kidneys, meaning of bodily exercise, structure and use of the skin, bathing, clothing, dwellings, foods and pleasures (under this intoxicating drinks, tobacco, etc.) Something regarding contagious diseases and help in times of accidents. Inject instruction on health when convenient in connection with the study of the organs of the body. Illustrate by experiment when possible. General review, especially the points concerning the nourishment and respiration of plants and animals.

The outline in nature study impresses one with the inclusiveness of the course. The elementary phases of animal life, plant life, physics, chemistry, and human physiology and health are made the objects of careful consideration. True this study in some cases is stiff, formal, meaningless, and without spirit because of not being connected with the vital interests of the pupils, but on the whole the work is brought very close home to their daily life. Through it the children are able to see the contributions to life and human welfare made by the innumerable things in man's environment.

Throughout the primary grades the work is mostly devoted to descriptive studies. Considerable attention is given also to the intrinsic value to man of animals, plants, and natural forces, and the means he has found for utilizing them in his struggle forward. The nature lessons throughout the grades are enriched and enlivened by the use of well selected and carefully prepared appliances and models for demonstration. Whenever possible the living animals and plants in their natural habitat, forces as applied in the machinery of neighboring institutions, and minerals in their successive processes of development and refinement are studied at first hand. Every school where the financial stringency is not too keen is provided with a liberal amount of apparatus for demonstrational purposes (*anskuelsesmidler*). As an instance, every primary school in the city of Christiania has at least one room of considerable size devoted exclusively to the storing of this material. Maps, charts, mounted specimens, plates, preserved articles, and accessory materials are there in abundance, and provide minute representations for most any point one might wish to make typical for illustration or study. The more genuine phases of laboratory work are not provided, though a considerable amount of crude experimentation is done in the grades.

g. Other subjects: writing and drawing, vocal music, manual training, gymnastics

The teacher presenting this course must be capable for he is the authority and guide back of all work done. Text books (good ones though condensed) play a part, but a much smaller part than would be the case in our American schools were similar instruction approached in a formal way. In other words, their teachers furnish the course and *teach* the subject, while too many of ours merely present the course provided in the adopted text book.

Writing, drawing, vocal music, manual training, and gymnastics are also in the curriculum and each receives careful attention. Perhaps extended outlining of these courses and long discussions concerning them are unnecessary. Their importance and value are recognized. Their presentation in the schools of Norway is commendable, but some things must be passed without exhaustive treatment. Only general statements will be given.

The results in some lines—writing and drawing in particular—do not justify the amount of time devoted to them. The writing is mechanical throughout, and in the lower grade the requirements are altogether too exacting. Drawing is required of all alike. Those who have ability in this line of work perhaps receive too little instruction; others, without talent or liking for it, regard it as a drudgery and, in the minds of some of their teachers, hinder the progress of the gifted. The finer coordinations required in both writing and drawing are frequently in advance of the development of the pupils and work injury rather than benefit.

Vocal music is required of all and injures none. Probably each one reaps considerable benefit from the instruction. The class of music used in their teaching is very different from what is in vogue in our American schools. The church has exercised a great deal of influence in this respect. Since church and state are united the music of the church forms a predominating portion of the music of the state schools. Psalms, chants, and songs of stately dignity constitute the bulk of their selections, while those of lighter strain are interspersed at intervals not too close together. In America our children's songs are more attractive from the "jingle" point of view. Our children like them better and are more anxious to sing them. The little Norwegians, too, are delighted when permitted to swing into the lighter strains of music. They love to sing. Their faces fairly glow as their mellow voices swell out whether they sing in a jingle or in the rich harmonies of their psalms. Common use of the better quality of music cultivates their ability to appreciate and to render works of higher order than one usually finds in the schools of our own country.

Manual and industrial training has had an important place in their schools for many years. Every hour spent at the bench is a delight to the boys, while the girls enjoy equally well the privilege of sewing or cooking. These activities are certainly valuable in the training of the young, and their influences extend into the homes of all the pupils.

Gymnastics is the regular order for all pupils. A Swedish system of exercises is used which requires little apparatus but yields large returns. Abundant well-directed exercises of various kinds are provided for every pupil at stated periods and are entered into with zest. The regularity with which the gymnastic exercises are given doubtless has much to do in preserving the health of the children. As a class they are not only free from weaknesses but are vigorous and robust. Another part of their gymnastic work is the outdoor exercise which is required of all the pupils between the class periods. This doubtless adds much life and animation to the entire school program.

The course as a whole includes the fundamentals and chief essentials to educational activity. Those who pass through the primary schools obtain an intelligent appreciation of life and its meanings. They are able to meet common needs successfully and to attend to general affairs in an approved manner. The masses feel the necessity of the fuller life thus provided and in turn the school is admirably fitted to the task of developing loyal and capable citizens. Furthermore, those who are so favorably situated that they may continue in school longer than seven years and desire fitness for entrance upon the work of higher education find in the primary schools every opportunity to gratify their desires.

The connection between the lower and higher schools was not at all satisfactory until 1896, when the Storthing readjusted the system. Since then pupils may pass regularly from the fifth grade of the primary school into the four year middle school, or after the completion of the seven grades of the primary school they may enter either a three or a four year middle school and finish in three years. Since the number desiring entrance to the middle school from the fifth grade is larger than can be accommodated, those of highest ranking educationally are admitted. While the secondary school men claim perfect right to choose the fittest for entrance into their schools, the primary school men feel that their work in the sixth and seventh grades suffers injustice as a result of this selective process. The connection between the schools is not yet perfect and some unrest is evidenced in reference to the matter. The chief need seems to be an increase in the number of middle schools.

III. THE MIDDLE SCHOOL

1. Its standard, aim, and method

The Storthing, in 1896, passed a law defining the limits and work of the middle school. According to the enactment this school builds upon the foundation laid in the primary school and secures to the pupils a thorough general education suited to the needs and receptivity of childhood. The course of study offered may be of varied length, but in no case shall it exceed four years in duration. The four year course aims at a very natural connection with the work done during the first five years in the common school. Where the connection can be made with the work of later grades in the primary school, the course of the middle school may be correspondingly shorter. The aim and methods are in general similar to those in the lower school; though, of course, higher, more thorough and inclusive, and such as give deeper insight into all subjects of instruction. It is required that instruction be given in religion, Norwegian, German, English, history, geography, natural science, mathematics, writing, drawing, manual training, and vocal music. Instruction in domestic economy may be provided for the girls.

2. Outline of subjects of instruction

Formerly all of these schools charged tuition; but, as the conditions in the commune gradually improved, provisions were made in some of them for the issuance of a certain number of free scholarships. These were usually governed in such a way that those most in need were the first to receive the benefits. From time to time scholarship funds were increased until now some communes provide free scholarships to all resident children. The city of Christiania has a three-year middle school building upon the foundation of seven years of primary work and charging no tuition whatsoever. This provision together with the building up of scholarship funds are forerunners of free entrance, probably, to all of the state's middle schools. As already stated, the work of the middle school overlaps in part that of the primary school. The course of study for Classes I and II is in a large measure a duplication of that provided for Classes VI and VII in the lower school. However, to present the work of the middle school adequately, it is essential that the course for the entire four years be here included. The state adopts a curriculum which is used in all of its secondary schools. Minor details such as texts vary in the different schools. The following is an outline of the curriculum used in the Christiania Cathedral School.

Religion

Class I. (Two hours.) Vogt's Bible History to the fall of the Kingdom of Judah. J. Sverdrup's Commentary to Article 2. Verses of hymns once each week.

Class II. (Two hours.) Vogt's Bible History from "The Exile" to "The Story of the Passion." Commentary from Article 2 to "The Sacraments." Verses from hymns.

Class III. (Two hours.) Bible History and Commentary completed and reviewed. Verses from hymns. Bible reading.

Class IV. (One hour.) Y. Brun and Th. Caspari's Church History gone through and reviewed. Cursory study of the ecclesiastical year and the order of divine service.

Here we note the beginnings of a more formal consideration of religion. A large part of the work is historical. Texts and lectures covering practically identical grounds form the basis of the work in this branch of study. The change to the more formal study of religion strikes the writer as a distinctive turn or transfer from moderately successful to useless endeavor. The personal touch and human flavor attending the informal telling of Bible stories afford some genuine inspiration. Life touches life. When character is exemplified in a living person or is shown through story once to have had expression in a fellow mortal, interest is awakened and the child instinctively imitates the vision before him. He transforms it into life. He enters into the spirit of the theme and the spirit giveth life.

On the other hand, when religion is presented in a formal way, when an abstract view is taken, when the core of the subject is in the cold pages of texts,—then the letter killeth. Through force of habit the children retain some respect for the wishes of the teacher and do go through the motions of study and recitation, but the life of the subject is very soon extinguished and even respect for it vanishes in large measure. However, in rare instances good results are obtained through the efforts of teachers who are especially well qualified for this work.

The Mother-Tongue and Old Norse

Class I. (Five hours.) Pauss and Lassen's Reader II. 2. Some of the Songs of the Fatherland learned by heart. Oral and written analysis. Hofgaard's Norwegian School Grammar, Paragraphs 1-31, 34-38, 41, 45, 48-59, 61, 65, 76-79. The more important part of Hougen's Rules for Correct Writing. Written work (dictation and composition) each week.

Class II. (Four hours.) Pauss and Lassen's Reader II. 3. Poems—among them some of the Songs of the Fatherland learned by heart. Hofgaard's Grammar continued, also analyses. One written exercise each week (dictation and easy composition.)

Class III. (Alternately three and four hours.) Pauss and Lassen's Reader III. Poems learned by heart—partly from Lassen's Poems for Middle Schools, partly from Songs of the Fatherland. Certain parts of the grammar reviewed. Analyses now and then. About twenty written exercises, among them some dictations.

Class IV. (alternating three and four hours.) Pauss and Lassen's Reader III. That portion from which the examination is taken, gone through and partly reviewed. Several poems committed to memory. Fourteen written exercises. Among the topics used the following are typical: The summer vacation, the location of our city, Denmark, past and present lighting systems, animal life in our forests, reminiscences from my earlier school days, birds and why we protect them, the Norsemen as seamen, Christiania in winter garb, Europe's natural conditions in preference to those of other continents.

In harmony with the indications of the plan of instruction, the early part of the work in the study of the mother-tongue is devoted to reading from selected texts. Simultaneously, grammar and rhetoric are carried along and put into use in written compositions which are frequent. Here, as in the primary schools, exact spelling, correct grammatical and rhetorical forms, and approved literary style are constant requirements. The child is expected not only to read intelligently, but to express himself orally and in writing in a comprehensive manner and in such form as to appeal to the intelligence of others. Thus both in oral speech and through written composition the pupil is privileged to put his attainments into continuous use. They acquire the tools of thought and skill in handling them.

German

Class I. (Six hours.) Knudsen and Kristiansen's Reader from the beginning to the "Subjunctive." Written exercises.

Class II. (Five hours.) Knudsen and Kristiansen's Reader from "Subjunctive" to close of book. Voss' Reader in section A, seventy-six pages, in section B, fifty pages; one-half of these shall be learned by heart. Hofgaard's Short German Grammar the most important forms. Written exercises. Rehearsals. Retroversions.

Class III. (Five hours.) Voss' Reader, in section A, seventy-five pages, in section B, fifty-eight. Hofgaard's Short German Grammar, inflections. In section B besides the above, paragraphs 140-148, 156, 169, 179-181. In addition section B shall have thirty-six pages of O. Kristiansen's oral exercises and thirty-two compositions according to O. Kristiansen's exercises in written work. In section A, written exercises, partly according to Kristiansen's outlines for written work and partly reviews of the lessons in the reading book.

Class IV. (Five hours.) Voss' Reader in section A, twenty pages, in section B, seventy-five. Repetition of the portion designated for minutest study. The grammar reviewed. One or two written exercises each week according to Kristiansen's outlines.

The instruction in German proceeds in a very natural manner. The earlier lessons are devoted very largely to oral instruction in which the teacher takes the lead. Words, phrases, and sentences are given by the teacher for translation and concert repetition. Repetition and concert work are prominent in many places in the schools, but nowhere stressed to the same extent as in their language instruction. Concert work seems to stimulate to freedom in pronunciation, while repetition affords the drill which is necessary to the required accuracy. Having had at least five years of thorough instruction in the mother-tongue the children are able to appreciate in a measure the meaning and importance of verb forms and other features of inflection so that they are ready to do consistent work in this phase of their study. In addition to the translations referred to, conversational exercises are soon introduced, and at the end of the second year some facility in easy conversation is evidenced. Toward the close of the middle school the children are able to read the language with ease and to converse in it quite fluently.

English

Class II. (Five hours.) Brekke's Elementary Reader to page seventy-four, studied and reviewed, besides the grammar in the back of the book. Conversational exercises and written work on the blackboard. During the last half year an occasional written exercise in a book.

Class III. (Five hours.) Brekke's Reader for the Middle School, sixty-five pages read and reviewed. Knap's Grammar. One narrative per week.

Class IV. (Five hours.) Brekke's Reader for the Middle School. Required portion read and reviewed, while the remainder of the book is gone through and in part read *ex tempore*. One narrative each week.

The study of English proceeds along lines parallel to those followed in the German. The learning of the language is accomplished chiefly through its use. Explanations are made by using the more familiar words of the tongue studied, by circumlocutions, and by other similar practices. Grammar is resorted to as a means rather than an end. It is used only in facilitating the acquisition of the language, not as an end in itself. However, at the close of the course each pupil has become quite proficient in the grammar as well as in reading the language and in conversing in it.

History

Class I. (Three hours.) Nissen's History of the World by Sehjoth, from the beginning until "Scandinavia in the Middle Ages."

Class II. (Two hours.) Text as in Class I. From "Scandinavia in the Middle Ages" to "Modern Times."

Class III. (Three hours.) Same Text. From "Charles V" to "The February Revolution." Review.

Class IV. (Three hours.) Same Text. Reviewed in its entirety.

The course in history is very rich and its study is entered into with animation. The teacher is usually a master in the subject and he makes the work of great profit. A considerable amount of the class period is devoted to a vivid and analytic introduction of the work to be done at the next meeting of the class, preparation for which shall be made in the meantime. Problems are presented and purposes are indicated so that the preparatory study may be done with some definite end in view.

All facts of history are placed in appropriate settings and perspective, correlated into a unity, and given vital meaning. Maps, charts, and pictorial illustrations are provided in abundance and used constantly. Frequently historic scenes near at hand or known to the pupils are pointed out, minutely described, and visited.

Teachers appeal to the sentiment of pupils with the aim of begetting loyalty for the fatherland in the hearts and minds of the young. I have heard instructors grow eloquent as they warmed up on phases of Norway's history, and have noted the flushed cheeks and snapping eyes of the children that bespoke the national pride of the young hearts as familiar words, slogans, and songs of their heroes were quoted.

When given an opportunity—a common occurrence—the pupils enter into the rehearsal of historic events with enthusiasm. Every mind in the room is active. They are awake to the situations and are familiar with the scenes and literature connected with the several stages of development. Replies given in response to questions from the teacher are nearly always in the form of narratives, sometimes occupying ten or fifteen minutes.

General history or history of any foreign country is entered into in a spirit similar to that characterizing the consideration of their own. On one occasion I listened to a review on American history. Among the characters taken up were Grant, Lee, Harriet Beecher Stowe, and Lincoln. The pupils discussed Uncle Tom's Cabin with familiarity, Lee was considered as "The Napoleon of America," but Lincoln was the one to whom most of the class period was devoted. At the close of the hour the teacher announced a lecture on "Abraham Lincoln" for the following Sunday evening in the Working-Men's College (*Arbeiderakademi*)[40] of which he was the director. This incident illustrates the way in which they correlate the work of different educational organizations, and shows their interest in the important events connected with the history of other nations.

Geography

Class I. (Two hours.) Arstal's Geography. Norway and Sweden. Review.

Class II. (Two hours.) Arstal's Geography. From "The Central European Mountains and Rivers" to "Asia." Studied and reviewed.

Class III. (Two hours.) Arstal's Geography. The foreign continents. Studied and reviewed.

Class IV. (Two hours.) Arstal's Geography. Repeated or reviewed in its entirety.

Two books are used in the study of this subject. One is made up entirely of well designed, carefully drawn, and thoroughly reliable maps, printed on a good quality of paper. The other is a text giving a good logical statement of what the course is calculated to include. The teacher must provide the major portion of the information by his own initiative and through cooperation of pupils. Illustrative material (*Anskuelsesmidler*) is provided in great abundance and in diversified variety.

An effort is made to impart to the pupils a satisfactory appreciation of the conditions prevailing in the countries considered. Their colonization, commerce, products, topography, political subdivisions, cities, population, river and mountain systems, climate, etc., are all carefully studied. The course begins with the geography of Norway. Next foreign lands and conditions are taken up and compared to situations at home. When the various countries on the globe have been kept for a time before the eyes, a thorough review is given which occupies the

[40] An organization providing a series of weekly lectures by men of prominence from various places, for the populace and especially adapted to the working classes.

greater portion of the last year in the middle school course.

Mathematics

Class I. (Five hours.) Numbers resolved into factors. Fractions. Some Proportion.

Class II. (Five hours.) Algebra: Bonnevie and Eliassen's text. From beginning to division. Geometry: Bonnevie and Eliassen's text. From beginning to right lines divided into equal parts. Arithmetic: Proportion and percentage.

Class III. (Five hours.) Algebra: Bonnevie and Eliassen's text. From division to equations with two unknowns. Geometry: Bonnevie's text. From parallelograms to Book IV. Drill in percentage and interest.

Class IV. (Five hours.) Algebra: Bonnevie and Eliassen's text. From equations with two unknowns to close of book. Geometry: Bonnevie's text. From Book IV to close of text. Review of entire text. Drill in computing solids and other miscellaneous problems. A few hours devoted to bookkeeping.

One of the most favorable features of their instruction in mathematics is the intimate connection they make between the several phases of the subject. Arithmetic, algebra, and geometry are never wholly separated from each other. They are in reality interwoven and so definitely correlated that each contributes to the others. By constant use the several processes become familiar tools in the mental activities of the pupils. Mastery of the principles of the science and ability in their use are the ends to be attained. The outline of the course indicates the extent of the field receiving attention. It is sufficient to say that the topics are all made to appear plain, definite, and vital; and that they are assimilated, and do become parts of the growing life.

Nature Study (Natural Science)

Class I. (Three hours.) Botany: Sorensen's text. Written descriptions of about twenty-five plant forms. Zoology: Vertebrates according to Sorensen's text.

Class II. (Two hours.) Botany: Sorensen's text. From "The Sunflower Family" to "Plant Structure." Plant analysis. Zoology: Sorensen's text. "Invertebrates." Review from treatise on insects to close of book.

Class III. (Two hours.) Zoology and botany reviewed. Plant analysis. Henrichsen's Physics. From beginning to "Properties of Air."

Class IV. (Three hours.) Henrichsen's Physics studied through and reviewed with related laboratory work. Knudsen and Falch's The Human Body I studied and reviewed.

The plan of work, as noted, includes botany, zoology, physics, and human physiology. Each subject is taken up and pursued in a consistent manner. In botany plant analysis and structure form the important part of the work. A herbarium is made by each pupil. The study is brought very definitely into the daily lives of the children with the intent of opening their eyes to the conditions in nature about them and of developing in them an appreciation of the almost unlimited provision made for man's welfare. Zoology and physiology are treated in a similar way. They are calculated to enrich the life of the individual by bringing him into more sympathetic relations with all living forms. In physics the child does some experimental work and thereby gets first hand experience to accompany, clarify, and assist in evaluating the elaborated instruction of the teacher regarding forces, phenomena, and laws.

It was interesting to note in a recitation chiefly devoted to experimental work that the language used in conversation was carefully scrutinized and that errors were corrected. Throughout the curriculum a very definite effort is made to utilize every phase of information possessed by the pupils.

IV. GYMNASIUM

1. Outline of subjects of instruction

Religion

Class I. (One hour.) Selected hymns, and chapters from the prophet Isaiah.

Class II. (One hour.) Short survey of church history. Brandrud's text used by some of the pupils.

Class III. (Two hours.) Short presentation of the Christian faith and ethics, without text. Survey of designated portions of John's Gospel, the Epistle to the Romans, and Revelations.

The instruction in religion is commonly given by the city pastors. While all of these men are highly educated, many of them lack the ability to awaken the minds of the pupils to an active interest in the subject. No examination in religion is required in the gymnasium. As a result of the formality in this teaching and the lack of incentives generally, the members of the classes are listless and inattentive. I insert a note that I made in reference to one class in which I was a visitor. "Most of the class was listless all of the time and all of them most of the time." I have on a few occasions heard short and irrelevant remarks made by pupils in response to direct questions by the instructor, and among the pupils it is accounted no reflection whatever if any of their number states that he knows nothing regarding the situation under discussion. The work appears altogether void of interest and without profit.

It seems almost pathetic that a subject of such importance should have its richness of content dissipated and wasted through lack of incentives or by reason of unsuccessful methods of presentation. My observation of the work from the beginning of the primary school through all the classes up to the completion of the gymnasium convinces me that the personal and concrete presentations in the lower grades are very successful but that the formal, authoritative work in the secondary schools is little more than failure.

Norwegian

Class I. A and B (Four hours.) Pauss and Lassen's Reader IV. 1. Njael's saga.

Holberg's The Busybodies and Peter Paars. Part of Ohlenschlager's Aladdin. Baggesen's Noureddin to Aladdin. Hertz's Svend Dyring's House. Also in A, Ibsen's Vikings at Helgeland; in B, Ibsen's The Feast at Solhaug; Bjornson's Synnove Solbakken.

Landsmaal. Garborg and Mortensen's Reader for Higher Schools. About forty pages from Aasen, Janson, Sivle, etc.

Fourteen compositions in each class. Assigned exercises: Impressions from the summer vacations; what do we learn from Njaal's saga regarding life and customs in Iceland about the year one thousand; a characteristic of the "Busybodies" by Holberg; Christiania as a city of manufacture and industry; a comparison between the east and west of Norway with references to nature and commerce; a painting I like; Norway as a tourist land; do not put off until tomorrow what you can do today; why could not the Persians conquer the Greeks; the dark sides of city life; what circumstances have combined in giving the Norsemen high ranking as seamen?

Class II. R. G. (Five hours.) History of Literature through the literature of the North, folk songs, a collection of Danish and Norwegian ballads, selections from Asbjornsen, Moe, and Holberg. Romance poetry, some read minutely and the rest cursorily. Consideration of Aasen and the Landsmaal movement. Sixty pages of Garborg and Mortenson's Landsmaal. About twenty pages of Old Norse from Nygaard's beginner's book.

Written exercises, frequently on topics of interest. Besides all this each pupil must give a discussion on a self-selected theme before the class.

Class II. L-H. (Six and five hours.) Holberg's Erasmus Montanus. Wessel's *Kjaerlighed uden Stromper* (Love without Stockings.) History of literature to about one thousand, eight hundred. Shakespeare's Julius Caesar. In the Landsmaal selections from Garborg and Mortenson's Reader (excepting folk songs.) Old Norse: Nygaard's beginner's book. Some pages from Thor to Utgard. Twelve written exercises on important literary, historical, and industrial subjects.

Class III. R. G. (Four hours.) History of literature from Holberg down to the present. Read scrutinizingly selected writings of Holberg, Ohlenschlager, Wergeland, Welhaven, Asbjornsen and Ibsen. In the Landsmaal read from Garborg and Mortenson's Reader and the writings of Vinje. In the Old Norse read the remainder of Nygaard's beginner's book. History of language and history of literature. Many written exercises, largely literary and historical topics.

Class III. L-H. (Five and four hours.) Special study of selections specified as examination material including the writings of Holberg, Wergeland, and Welhaven. Landsmaal from Garborg and Mortenson's Reader. History of Literature. History of Language. Twelve written compositions on important topics.

The work in literature throughout the gymnasium deals with the masterpieces of the language in an analytic and critical way. The aims are to familiarize the pupils with the best productions in the language, to acquaint them with the lives and historical relations of their authors, and to develop literary appreciation and style.

Accordingly many writers are included, translations of world classics are utilized, history of literature in its connections with general history receives attention, and ability in composition is encouraged and required.

Eddas, sagas, and the more important productions from successive periods are studied in minute detail. The Landsmaal is not neglected. When any piece of literature is under discussion, related historical events; references to other literary productions, characters, myths, etc.; the life of the author; and many other important points are considered exhaustively. The intricacies of the language are sought out in patience and made familiar. Every known device for completing the literary background is utilized. Since the literature of the country is a part of the life of its citizens, no effort is required to secure intense interest in the work.

In the linguistic-historical course more time is devoted to this branch of instruction than is given to it in the *real* and Latin courses. The quality or class of work is essentially the same though the quantity is necessarily less in the two latter courses. A definite effort is made to place each pupil in possession of the culture represented in the national literature.

German

Class I. A and B (Three hours.) Gundersen's German for the Gymnasiums. A, sixty-seven pages, B, seventy-five pages, consisting of the following titles: *Die Sanger, Die Burgschaft, Der Ring des Polykrates Der Handschuh, Die Sonne Bringt es an den Tag, Die Goldene Repetieruhr, Wie der Meisenseppe Gestorben ist, Umzingelt, Der Stumme Ratsherr, Zur Geschichte des 30-jahrigen Krieges, Landsknecht and Soldat.* In B review the more important features of syntax in O. Kristiansen's Grammatical Exercises.

Once every week a written review of a lesson read.

Class II. (Three hours.) Gundersen's German for Gymnasiums, about one hundred pages. Fifteen written exercises, partly reproductions of new matter and partly write-ups of what has been studied. In *real* gymnasium some supplementary assignments in addition (*Das Schneeschuhlaufen, Die Lage Kristianias,* etc.)

Class III. (Alternating three and four hours.) Gundersen's German for Gymnasiums. Reading finished and the greater part of it reviewed. Every second week a written review covering two consecutive hours.

German is recognized as the language of a great neighbor nation and is assiduously studied. Much time has been spent in the middle school in acquiring the language and now three years are used in introducing the pupils into the thought-life and culture of the nation through the inner contact of its literature. Some of Germany's more important authors are studied rather exhaustively. An endeavor is also put forth to become familiar with the most remarkable events in the history of that Empire. Through this advanced treatment they perfect their knowledge of the language as such, and further their ability to converse in the foreign tongue.

French

Class I. A (Four hours.) After the more important parts of phonology, Hermanstorff and Wallem's Reader in French for the Gymnasium I. pp. 18-108. The most essential parts of the grammar, together with many exercises in translation. While reviewing, special emphasis is placed upon reading exercises.

Class I. B (Four hours.) Hermanstorff and Wallem's Reader I pp. 1-55 read and reviewed, together with the corresponding translations from Norwegian p. 109 ff. In addition pages 98-108 are read and reviewed and most of the remaining exercises are gone through cursorily. Wallem's Vocabulary Part I. 1 and Part V. 6-9 are studied.

Class II. R. G. (Two hours.) Hermanstorff and Wallem's Reader II pp. 1-31 and 104-112. Grammar drill by references to synopses of grammar in the beginner's book. Wallem's Vocabulary Part I. 1 and V. 6-10 studied and reviewed.

Class II. Lang. (With Latin five hours, without Latin four hours.) Hermanstorff and Wallem's Reader. Division without Latin about eighty pages, consisting of Part I., the last section and Part II selections for A, I-VI for B, III, IV, VII, XI. Division with Latin, the same amount excepting B, VII and XI. Wallem's Vocabulary, review V. 6-9.

Class III. R. G. (Two hours.) Hermanstorff and Wallem's Reader, about eighty pages.

Class III. Lang. (Three hours.) Hermanstorff and Wallem's Reader I, the last section and II for A, I-X and for B, I-XIII with the exception of a few selections such as X in A which is read only cursorily. As exercise in *ex tempore* translation use Duruy's History of France.

About the same amount of French is taken in the Latin as in the *real* course of study though it is carried but for two years in the former and three in the latter.[41] More time is provided for it in the linguistic-historical course then in either of the others. Reference to the table on page 171 will indicate exactly the amount of time used and its distribution throughout the years.

The French language is not as closely related to the Norwegian as are the German and English. Greater variations are noted both in pronunciation and in vocabulary. Almost universally the Norwegians regard it as the most difficult of the three foreign languages to acquire.

The study of French is not begun until the pupils enter the gymnasium when they are fourteen or fifteen years old. English and German are begun three and four years before French. The teachers believe that a mistake is made in not beginning the study of French earlier. It is worthy of note that the Norwegian pedagogues who have tried beginning instruction in the languages at different times in the school course are definitely of the opinion that to begin the study of a foreign language early is a distinct advantage. It seems to the writer that American schools might profit by this experience and introduce the study of languages in the lower grades.

---

[41] The course with Latin includes 4 hours of French in the first year and 5 hours in the second; the *real* course offers it 4 hours in the first year, and 2 hours in the second and third years.

TABLE XI

Course of study showing weekly hours in Christiania Cathedral School (1910-1911).

	GYMNASIUM												
COURSES	*Real*		LANGUAGE-HISTORY				LATIN			MIDDLE SCHOOL			
CLASSES	3	2	1	3	2	1	3	2	1	IV.	III.	II.	I.
Religion	2	1	1	2	1	1	2	1	1	1	2	2	2
Norwegian	4	5	4	5	6	4	4	5	4	3½	3½	4	5
German	3½	3	3	3½	3	3	3½	3	3	5	5	5	6
French	2	2	4	3	4	4	0	5	4				
English	2	2	4	7	7	4	2	2	4	5	5	5	
Latin							11	7					
History	3	3	3	5	5	3	3	3	3	3	3	2	3
Geography	2	1	1	2	1	1	2	1	1	2	2	2	2
Mathematics	6	6	4	2	2	4	2	2	4	5	5	5	5
Natural Science	5	5	4	1	1	4	1	1	4	3	2	2	3
Writing										½	½	1	2
Drawing	1	2	2			2			2	2	2	2	2
Vocal Music	1	1	1	1	1	1	1	1	1		1	1	1
Gymnastics	4	4	4	4	4	4	4	4	4	4	3	3	3
Manual Training										2	2	2	2
Total	35½	35	35	35½	35	35	35½	35	35	36	36	36	36

English

Class I. (Four hours.) Brekke and Western's Selections from English Authors for the First Gymnasium. The regulation sixty pages (matter from which examination is taken) is read and reviewed. Forty pages *ex tempore*. One synopsis or reproduction each second week. Knudsen's English Prepositions and Synonyms.

Class II. R. G. and Latin (Two hours.) Brekke and Western's Selections for Second and Third Classes in the *Real* Gymnasium. Sixty-seven pages read and reviewed in part. *Ex tempore*: Called Back of Conwoy.

Class II. L-H. (Seven hours.) Brekke and Western's Selections from English Authors for Second and Third Linguistic-Historical Classes, one hundred and sixty pages. Merchant of Venice, Act I. Most of Brigadier Gerard by Conan Doyle. Western's English Institutions gone through. Otto Anderssen's History of Literature to "Bacon." Written exercises each week.

Class III. R. G. (Two hours.) Anderssen and Eitrem's Selection of English Classics, thirty-three pages. The portion from which selections are taken for the final examination (*Artium Examen*) reviewed in its entirety. *Ex tempore*: Called Back of Conwoy.

Class III. L-H. (Seven hours.) Brekke and Western's Reader. Obligatory, Selections 3, 4, 16, 17, 11, 19. From Otto Anderssen's English Literature the required amount: Swift, Byron, Thackeray, Merchant of Venice. O. Anderssen's History of English Literature. Western's English Institutions. Written work each week.

Class III. Latin (Two hours.) Anderssen and Eitrem's Selection of English Classics, forty-five pages. Review of selections from which examinations are taken.

The connections the Norwegians sustain with the English speaking world are, perhaps, stronger than those binding them to any other people. Norway has close commercial associations with both England and America, and rarely does one find a family in Norway without near relatives in one or both countries. As a consequence, more than usual interest attaches to the study of English. Strenuous efforts are now being made to introduce it into the curriculum of the elementary school, and such change will probably be effected at an early date.

According to the present plan those who graduate from the gymnasium have studied English six or seven years and have gained a fairly definite knowledge of it. They are able to read fluently and converse with ease. They have become familiar also with much of the best English literature, and through it have been brought into close touch with the life and culture of the English speaking peoples.

Latin

Class II. Latin (Seven hours.) Schreiner's Short Grammar. Inflection and some of the rules of syntax. Ording's elementary book. Ording's Latin Reading Selections, pp. 1-36. Written exercises each week.

Class III. Latin (Eleven hours.) Schreiner's Latin Reading Selections, pp. 30-67 and 73-88. Livy XXII., chapters 4, 9-15, 16-18, 19-28, 42-55. Cicero in Verrem IV., sections 1-14, 60-70, 72-81, 105-115. Schreiner's Short Grammar: Syntax. Forty written translations.

Latin is included in the curricula of only about one-half of the gymnasia of Norway.[42] It is taught by competent teachers who appeal to the interests of the pupils through related history and literature, and through promise of linguistic excellence. The work is gone into thoroughly, drill is constant, and readiness in response is demanded.

Despite the excellent quality of instruction there is a general feeling among the Norwegians that the study of Latin does not yield the immediate and substantial returns coming from other kinds of study. While they recognize that for advanced work in certain lines Latin is a prerequisite, they are convinced that, outside of those special lines of learning, contemporary tongues, history, biology, industrial chemistry, and other scientific subjects are more beneficial. As a consequence this branch of study is on the decline.

History

Class I. (Three hours.) Ancient history as treated in Raeder's text. History of the middle ages up to the second division from Schjoth and Lange's General History.

Class II. R. G. and Latin (Three hours.) Schjoth and Lange's General History. History of the Middle Ages and of Modern times until the Vienna Congress. History of Scandinavia until 1720. Survey of its more important portions—oral or written.

Class II. L-H. (Five hours.) History of the Middle ages down to the French Revolution from Schjoth and Lange's General History. History of Scandinavia to 1720. In addition use two hours per week in historical readings including such topics as the feudal system, medieval poetry, the university, Venice, craftsmen and merchants in the middle ages, Fredrik II., Hanseatics and aristocracy in the north, William Pitt.

Class III. L-H. (Five hours.) Schjoth and Lange's General History finished. Scandinavian history in the nineteenth century. Review of all requirements. Taranger's Social Conditions or Civics. Historical readings including introduction to the French Revolution, state rights in Norway, general culture and political development in our time, Norway in 1814, historical events.

Class III. Real and Latin. (Three hours.) History of Norway since the treaty of Kiel in 1814, and the history of Europe after the Vienna Congress, using Schjoth and Lange's General History. The more important features are presented in oral synopses. Besides this Taranger's Civil Government of Norway.

The study of history in the gymnasium builds very definitely upon the foundations laid in the primary and middle schools. The supposition is that the pupils are by this time capable of getting from texts the information they contain.

The class periods are devoted partially to texts of lesson preparation, but mostly to free discussion and to presentation of relevant material by the instruc-

[42] A school law passed in 1896 omitted Latin from the course of study. Another act of the same Storthing granted privilege of offering Latin as an elective in several schools.

tor. Bits of information regarding the private life of historical characters, minor incidents in their careers, and varied personal touches given by the teacher infuse spirit and vitality into the entire course. The lessons are brought directly home to the pupils and they are able to appreciate the fact that they are inheritors of past accomplishments and participants in present activities. Some of the most interesting and enthusiastic recitations I visited were in history.

All through the course in history Norway is given first attention and consideration. Its history is begun first, all along it is made the center around which the history of other nations is grouped, and finally it is given the concentrated, mature, and crowning efforts of those pursuing the long course of instruction. The closing year is generally devoted to a study of social and political conditions in the fatherland. Norway's constitution with its many provisions and administrative features of government (general and local) is given to the youths in clear, concrete, and concise presentations. Upon leaving the gymnasium the young people, therefore, are in a position to appreciate the meaning, privileges, and responsibilities of citizenship. While they have their affections centered in their native land, they are able to comprehend the relative accomplishments, standing, and conditions of other countries.

Geography

Class I. (One hour.) Haffner's Physical Geography.

Class II. (One hour.) Steen's Mathematical Geography. Completed and reviewed.

Class III. (Two hours.) Arstal's Economic Geography. Review all requirements.

The gymnasial course in geography includes physical geography, astronomy, and political geography. It is rich and profitable. Under the head of physical geography are included such topics as physiography, petrography, dynamic geology, history of the world's development, the earth's surface, oceanography, and the atmosphere. While only a general survey of the respective fields is possible, the pupils obtain a pretty fair grasp of fundamentals and feel that they have a very good and adequate idea of what their home—the earth—really is.

The work in astronomy or mathematical geography, as it is frequently called, is concerned chiefly with the earth's place in the universe, the Copernican system, Keppler's laws, the moon, the earth (form, size, and motion), the celestial world in general, the sun's apparent motion, the sun as a measurer of time, etc., etc.

Political geography provides acquaintance with the earth in special reference to man's presence and welfare. It treats of his means of livelihood, ways of communication, and the conditions under which he colonizes, builds up cities, and develops generally.

Mathematics

Class I. (Four hours.) Algebra: Bonnevie and Berg's text. From beginning to "Series." Geometry: Bonnevie and Sorensen's text. Entire text covered and reviewed. Examples at home and at school.

Class II. Real (Six hours.) Algebra: Bonnevie and Berg's text. From "Series" to end of text. Trigonometry: Johannesen's text. Completed and reviewed. Stereometry: Guldberg's text. Completed and reviewed. Analytical Geometry: Guldberg's text. From beginning to "The Ellipse." Problems at home and at school.

Class II. Linguistic (Two hours.) Algebra: Bonnevie and Berg's text. "Series." Trigonometry: O. Johannesen's text. Solving of problems.

Class III. Real (Six hours.) Guldberg's Analytical Geometry. E. Holst's Higher Arithmetical Series. Review of all requirements in *real* course. Solution of problems.

Class III. Linguistic (Two hours.) Review of the entire requirement. Examples at home and at school.

In addition to completing the work begun in the middle school in arithmetic, algebra, and geometry; instruction in the gymnasium includes trigonometry, stereometry, analytical geometry, and higher arithmetical series. The methods of instruction are the same as those used in the middle school though, of course, adapted to the greater maturity and stronger mentality of the pupils. By the time pupils enter the gymnasium considerable ability should have been gained in working independently. Where necessary, the teacher cooperates in solving problems and makes sure that the principles involved are thoroughly understood.

Frequently during the recitation period several members of the class are called to the blackboard, one at a time, to perform operations under consideration. As the pupil develops the problem he explains every step taken as he proceeds. The other pupils observe closely, take notes, and offer suggestions. The instructor carefully supervises every move, giving explanations when necessary not permitting erasures or leaving any operation until all in the class understand fully. In this way hearty cooperation is secured. Every mind is actively engaged and the excellent results testify of the validity of the method.

Work in analytical geometry and higher arithmetical series is taken only by those in the *real* course of instruction.

Natural History

Class I. (Four hours.) Chemistry: Waage's The Chemistry of Daily Life. Gone through and reviewed. Physiology: Knudsen and Falch's The Human Body II. Studied and reviewed.

Class II. Real (Five hours.) Isaachsen's Physics. From the beginning to "Heat." Review after having carefully studied. Exercises at home and at school. Botany: Th. Resvoll's text. Completed and reviewed.

Class II. Linguistic (One hour.) Botany: Resvoll's text. Completed and reviewed.

Class III. Real (Five hours.) Isaachsen's Physics. From "Heat" to end of text. Entire text reviewed. Zoology: Chr. Bonnevie's text. Studied and reviewed. Botany: Th. Resvoll's text reviewed.

Class III. Linguistic (One hour.) Zoology: Chr. Bonnevie's text. Studied and reviewed. Botany: Th. Resvoll's text reviewed.

Natural Science or Nature Study in the earlier years of school life is less differentiated than it becomes in the gymnasium. Here we find the fields very definitely separated. The more important chemical laws, animal and vegetable development and growth (botany and zoology), and the more essential features of human physiology and hygiene form centers of attention throughout the three years. In the *real* course physics also is stressed, though in the other courses of study little time is provided for it.

Not as much is made of the laboratory method as seems advisable. While every school has some provision for it they do not go at it in real earnest. Only one or two at a time can do first hand work. The others cooperate mentally and get some benefit, but they cannot reap the greater results which immediate individual experimentation yields.

One day during the progress of a lesson in zoology (where I was a visitor) a supply of live specimens arrived from the marine biological station at Drobak, and the remaining portion of the hour was devoted to investigations at close range. Interest was intense. Pupils dipped in (literally) and investigated at their own pleasure quite informally. The material was soon divided up into several receptacles, and around each of these gathered an eager group in an effort to use, handle, and examine every specimen. Those who had no interfering appointments for the succeeding hour accounted it a great favor to be privileged to continue this study for an extra class period. This is but one illustration of the interest attending laboratory work where each pupil may handle and examine for himself—where he may be a doer, an active participant instead of merely an observer.

CHAPTER IV

INTERPRETATIVE CONCLUSIONS

This chapter is for the consideration of some of the more important phases of the school system presented in greater detail in the foregoing chapters. The aim is to bring some features of Norway's system under close inspection, to interpret them in the light of commonly accepted pedagogical principles, to make comparisons between them and our own, and to suggest possible improvements where they seem to be needed. It is clearly evident that school practices admirably adapted to the social conditions in one country may be far from desirable in another. On the other hand, it is well-known that some educational means may be equally suitable in more than one country. Furthermore, certain fundamental principles are effectual wherever education is attempted. We shall hope to find some things worthy of being adopted bodily by us and others capable of transformation into shapes calculated to improve our educational practices.

1. THE PEOPLE AND THEIR IDEALS

The Norse are a sturdy race having potentialities capable of great accomplishment when once aroused and rightly directed. Conditions prevented these capacities from functioning with freedom until the middle of the last century when the store of energy which had accumulated during preceding decades and centuries asserted itself and effected a rapid rise in the political and intellectual status of the nation.

It is believed that Norway is now in a period of transition from a condition of mediocrity to one of eminence among the nations of the world. Politically, ethically, and educationally she assumes larger proportions daily.

As individuals the Norwegians are recognized among the leaders in literature, art, and science, and equal to any as pioneers in the development of the rich frontiers. As citizens they are enthusiastically welcomed everywhere. Climatic conditions and habits of life have given them the sturdiness of physique and vigor of mind which make them fearless and undaunted in the face of great undertakings and critical situations. They have become habituated to overcoming all obstacles in their way, and they naturally concentrate their energies for the achievement of their desired ends.

It is reasonable to expect similar traits in them as a nation. Their past actions declare these same tendencies and their present attitudes confirm the observer in the belief that the history of Norway will continue the story of regular and ever higher development. Their strongly democratic individuality seems to have been a factor in enabling them to realize and recognize their self in a very successful way. Matters of importance put the entire state into action and it ploughs through to the bottom of things. While very conservative, the state will not permit precedent to stand in the way of accepting new conditions when they are proven superior to the old. After thorough examination of every detail it passes judgment on the situation and then stands on that solution. Conservation has been an operating principle with them all along the line. A step in advance, some worthy achievement, new or loftier ideals, greater political freedom, and the like when once gained are always retained.

The union of church and state for example has been to their advantage. Matters of religion and politics were handled by the same hands and as a consequence both were strengthened. Each found in the other sources of inspiration and power. They both recognized education as a necessary fundamental means for their preservation and advancement. Acting in the main on the educational ideals of Martin Luther the church accepted the chief responsibilities in the direction of school activities, while the state very cheerfully undertook the burden of their support. Through the processes of growth direct responsibilities have been more and more shifted to the state, though the church continues to exert very strong influence and render every possible assistance.

Resulting from this cooperative activity a system of education has evolved which is effectual in the improvement of the state and in the maintenance of the noblest ideals of the church. According to its design this system of schools qualifies all children in the land for intelligent citizenship, and prepares them severally for the performance of every function of state, the service of the church, and for the various arts, professions, and other occupations of life. In other words, Norway provides for her children educational advantages suitable to every legitimate requirement or desire. Thus its school system develops a loyal, well-trained citizenship capable of maintaining its highest ideals and eager to cooperate in moving the fatherland forward into greater and nobler achievement.

2. FACILITIES FOR EDUCATION

To satisfy the varied requirements of the nation along the line of educational facilities it has been necessary to establish a complex system of diversified schools. Fundamental in the system are the *primary schools* providing the thorough elementary training so essential and effectual in the qualifying of citizens. Following these are the *secondary schools*—middle school and gymnasium—which afford the advantages of higher education along the more liberal lines. Besides these are the many institutions—public and private—for technical and professional study. There are general technical schools, schools of trades and manual arts, agricultural and horticultural institutions, naval and military academies, schools of art, teachers' colleges, a technical high school—an engineering college and institute of technology of high rank—in the city of Trondhjem, and the Royal Frederik University in Christiania which is devoted to specialized study and research in science, letters, and learned professions, including theology, law, medicine, and education. The last is provided for in the affiliated Pedagogical Seminary recently established.

At this point we may speak a word in commendation of the important part played by private institutions in Norway. Among them may be enumerated primary and secondary schools, teachers' seminaries, and technical institutes. Being of high merit and operating side by side with the state schools, they have rendered valuable service and exerted a wholesome influence. The state has recognized their work and expressed its appreciation of their efforts by giving them standing and by voting annuities to certain of them.

The uniformly high standard of preparation required for entrance to and the close correlation between the several special schools make easy the passage from one to another when it is desired, and give solidarity and unity wherein cooperation is natural and mutually beneficial.

It should be noted that provision is made for the proper care of the exceptional child in Norway. This is more particularly true of the defective. The child who is dull of comprehension along some lines receives individual assistance from his regular teacher or another who is employed to do the work. Recognition is given to disparity in physiological and mental age of children. Those who are definitely lacking in mentality are segregated into classes in the large schools and into separate schools in the larger cities, where they are provided with abundant, well-selected equipment and expert teachers who exert every effort to improve the conditions and to overcome the handicaps of the unfortunates. Morally delinquent children are placed in children's homes—homes for correction—where they are supervised and taught. Each child is placed under the conditions best suited to his needs—where he will be most profited. All of this work comes under the authority of the school officials, and as a result there is close coordination between the regular and the special schools.

Not only do these officials care for the mentally and morally delinquent but they are also authorized and required to take children from environments that are likely to develop evil and lawless traits. Unfit parents may be deprived of the control and authority over their offspring who are taken and placed in private homes of moral influence or in children's homes where they receive proper care and training. Being vested with such authority the school officials are able to do much toward the prevention of delinquency as well as to attend specifically to the individual cases where a lack of moral responsibility is evidenced.

Here are wholesome lessons for our American schools. Instead of giving sufficient individual help or providing expert teachers for the less intelligent, we permit them to become repeaters or to drop out altogether; in place of taking the child from an evil environment before he becomes a moral delinquent and placing him under moral surroundings in some good home, we hesitate to interfere with parental rights—as though they were greater than social—and permit him to become a law-breaker; and rather than give to school officials the authority and necessary equipment to care rightfully for the child who has committed some error, we place him in the hands of the law and he is probably sent to a reformatory having neither facility for his proper treatment nor any connection with the schools whatsoever.

Closer co-ordination of these educational functions and institutions would prevent much misfortune, cure a vast amount of misery, and accomplish more efficient results.

3. DIRECTING AUTHORITY AND MANAGEMENT OF SCHOOLS

Norway's educational authority is definitely centralized in the person at the head of the Department of Ecclesiastical and Educational Affairs, who is a member of the King's cabinet. The several departments, bureaus, commissions, and boards for control are radiations from this central focus. Furthermore, their schools are parts and parcels of one very definite, though somewhat complex, system; each class of schools, in its respective field, is ordered according to certain specifications; and all are coordinated so as to result in a unified whole without overlapping, or exposure of ragged and loose ends.

The controlling features of greater importance such as curriculum, appointment of teachers, plans of instruction, and the determination of qualifications for teaching positions are in the hands of the higher authorities. In effect the state determines the policies, the officers are expected to respect them, and the patrons exercise but little direct control. For example, the law provides that completion of certain grades of school work shall mean practically the same throughout the country, that the middle school and gymnasium examinations shall be uniform everywhere in the state, that standards of academic fitness for teaching positions must be the same, and that teachers' salaries shall not be below a certain minimum amount. Local opinion never has a thought of departing from these requirements.

Being vested with considerable authority the school officials are able not only to make suggestions and recommendations, but also to enforce all school regulations. This plan is successful in securing the most efficient service of which the officials are capable. They are expected to pursue their duties and perform their obligations according to directions without being too largely influenced by the opinions of individuals or community sentiment. Local politics plays a very small part in determining what shall be the educational trend, though the patrons of the school do enjoy considerable liberty and bear some responsibilities in arranging minor factors with reference to local situations.

We Americans might avoid a vast amount of leakage and unnecessary expenditure by improved organization of our educational institutions. A unified system of education, manned by competent officials with some authority, might easily raise the standard of efficiency of our schools several grades, and at the same time reduce the proportional cost. President Hall has given optimistic expression along this line. He writes:—"The time is not far off when we shall coordinate all educational agencies for all classes of children of school age.... All... institutions for the care and betterment of the bodies, minds or morals of children should correlate their work so that eventually it may all become so consolidated that each child can be placed in that position in the whole great system which will do most and best for it at each stage and so that changes from one to the other can be made whenever it becomes for the welfare of the child.... Diversities of agencies, aims and method should increase; and incorrigibles, defectives, homeless, neglected, backward children and the rest should each have special provision; but integration should keep pace with this differentiation."[43]

Were our public schools, reformatories, schools for defectives, etc., etc., all combined into one system they might perform their offices more effectively than they do now. Instead of permitting each to run along independent of the rest, they should be made to supplement each other.

Again, it is a matter of common knowledge that in our own country high school graduation, qualifications for teaching positions in the several grades of school work, college entrance requirements, college degrees, etc., are without uniform standardization. At present even a college degree has meaning only when the work and equipment of the institution granting it have been carefully estimated; state teachers' certificates may or may not be valid in other states; and reciprocity among the states in recognizing certificates is not in operation generally. While state certificates are not always demanded, some of the states are now requiring that all teachers in the high schools must be college graduates. In all too many instances the only effectual prerequisite to obtaining a position as teacher in the schools—primary or secondary—is the vote of the school directors. The gradation of educational activity according to a fixed basis and the raising of standards in academic and pedagogical preparation and in personal fitness for teaching positions would make the schools vastly greater factors in the country's progress and do the nation an inestimable service.

Centralization and uniformity in authority and purpose are distinctly evident in every school activity in Norway. The authority of the state is clearly stamped on the work of every official from the directing head to the last in position. Everyone connected with the system feels the obligations of the position occupied and, at the same time, recognizes his own security while keeping within the limits of the law. They all concentrate their energies in an earnest endeavor to realize the ends which the educational system is designed to reach. Even individual subjects of instruction are presented for specific purposes which in turn contribute to the general end to be reached through the course of study as a whole. Purposes, aims, and ends are always in the foreground of attention, and when teacher and pupils cooperate and are actuated by common ideals, their efforts are sure to be vital and successful.

4. TEACHERS' TRAINING

Proper pedagogical training is perhaps the most potent factor for good in educational activity. But few systems, if any, adequately meet the needs along this line. Some are well supplied with institutions devoted to the training of teachers

[43] Hall, G. Stanley, Educational Problems. Vol. I. p. 294.

so far as their number and distribution are concerned but they are lacking in quality; others have training schools very high in quality but they are poorly distributed and insufficient in number.

The ideals and equipment of these special institutions are factors of prime importance in determining their real values. These center in the personnel of the directing and teaching force. Too frequently thorough scientific preparation for the specific work of supervising and instructing in teachers' seminaries is wanting. Natural endowment coupled with long, varied, and successful experience has been regarded as sufficient qualification. To be sure, native ability is an absolute essential; experience is of immeasurable value; but intensive scientific research in the fields of child nature and development, psychology, and pedagogical principles, together with scientific methods, are equally indispensable.

Now it is a truism that teachers teach as they have been taught. Hence, to achieve greatest results, prospective teachers should secure their education (general and professional) from ideal teachers as far as possible and obtain experience through practice teaching under the personal supervision of masters in education. Preparing under such conditions, their natural capabilities would be brought more nearly to maximum efficiency and they would become powers for good in the profession. To have seminaries so distributed and equipped that all prospective teachers might have the best training within easy access would be an ideal condition.

Germany affords an unparalleled example in the development of teachers' seminaries. No other nation ever had a system of training schools as efficient as the one there provided. Her right to the title of "School mistress of the world" is in large measure traceable to the excellent training provided for and required of the teachers in the schools.

Norway early recognized the importance of this phase of school work and established six teachers' seminaries. Subsequently four private seminaries have been opened and the state has instituted the Pedagogical Seminary in affiliation with the university in Christiania. This gives them a liberal number of training colleges well distributed. While they are subject to some adverse criticism for failure to keep pace with the development of their school system as a whole, we must admit that the excellent results achieved by the schools of Norway are due largely to the early provision of these seminaries and insistence upon special training for teaching positions.

It is probable that certain normal schools of the United States deserve the honors so far as ideals and results are concerned even though we have accorded first ranking in system to Germany. Our plan, however, is too individual in nature to accomplish greatest good. We lack a centralized authority with power to do things. We have practically no co-ordination between state systems and no uniformity. Even in certain states the several schools do not cooperate or supplement each other as they should. The waste occasioned by the looseness of our system is enormous. Could we unify our resources, systematize our equipment, and provide efficient direction along cooperative lines of activity, the American schools would advance by leaps and bounds such as have not been known up to the present time in any nation.

A word is in place here with reference to the process of obtaining professional preparation. One of the best things to be gained by special training is a professional attitude toward the work of teaching. This cannot be attained by spasmodic effort but must be grown into. It comes rather as a result of long-continued study and application of principles than by intensive training for a short while. Direct instruction and experiment extended over a long period of time affords opportunity for innumerable associations and interrelations which no "hurry-up" process can provide. When professional training and study along the general lines of academic learning parallel each other they become interwoven in such a way that each contributes to the other, and simultaneously the proper attitude with respect to educational processes becomes a very real part of the student's life.

There are a number of important pedagogical principles which should become ingrained in the life of the individual in order that he make a success in the teaching profession. It is a generally conceded and commonly practiced rule in education that to thoroughly master any field of knowledge and really get into its vital parts it is necessary to keep the mind acting upon it, at least intermittently, through several years of time. Principles acted and reacted upon, viewed in this light and that, examined under a certain condition and then another, and tested in various ways may result very differently in one's life than when given a hurried, even though intensive, examination. They are certain in the one instance to sink deep into the life of the individual while in the other case they may or may not affect his behavior.

It seems, therefore, that if the excellent features which now characterize Norway's Pedagogical Seminary might be carried along through the whole or a large part of the college course, or if the work of the seminary might be supplemented by studies such as principles of education, history of education, child study, and psychology, carried along with the college work the results would be more effectual—the preparation for teaching more thorough. However, considering the short time that has elapsed since the founding of this Seminary, its work is of high order and its ideals are praiseworthy. The expressed intent of the director is to develop the field as rapidly as possible until it shall be characterized by the best means of professional training known to the science.

5. THE TEACHERS' LIFE

The life of the teacher is one of service, calling for an expenditure of the self to an extent perhaps greater than any other profession. Among the Norse, however, it is not as strenuous as that experienced in American schools. The Norwegian teachers have more time than we for recreation, self-improvement, or any of the activities opened up by leisure hours. Life generally is set at a more moderate pace with the Norsemen than with the rushing Americans, and the schoolmen enjoy the attendant advantages along with those in other professions or occupations.

While leisure among certain classes leads to idleness and corruption, it has quite opposite results among the better class of citizens. Windelband says that "The cultured man is he who in his leisure does not become a mere idler." The cultured men of the past have in their leisure developed science, art, literature, and philosophy. They have had reserve energy after the performance of their regular labors to use in fruitful, self-selected activities. There are always innumerable avenues through any one of which an earnest servant of the state may bring great gain to its people.

There is no nobler profession than that devoted to the development of youth; neither is there any occupation which brings more satisfying recompenses. The child is the most precious asset of the nation and deserves the maximum service possible for teachers to render. To perform the most efficient service the teacher should have health, vigor, and time for recreation in addition to scholastic and professional qualifications. When school authorities make conditions conducive to these ends, the results will be of such character that teachers, pupils, patrons, and community will all obtain greater profits.

Where school activities are not overtaxing, the teacher has opportunity to build up his physical being, increase the buoyancy of his spirits so as to enthuse his pupils to a greater extent, or improve his educational qualifications. One may concentrate his efforts along some given line of research and from day to day give the pupils under his tuition the benefits derived from these specialized efforts. An individual by persistent study may become the discoverer of new laws or truths which reach the ends of the earth and profoundly influence human affairs. Whatever the particular activity, leisure consecrated to the uplift of mankind is sure to result in great good.

When institutions drive their servants to the limit of their powers they must inevitably be the losers in the long run. They extinguish the light of ambition, reduce to machines the individuals who should be contributors to human progress, and make legion "the man with the hoe." Such practice in our schools results in waste of energy, depletion of our teaching force, and irretrievable loss in many ways.

It is my candid opinion that the rapidity of the evolution of the Norwegian school system, its excellencies, and the highly satisfactory results coming from it are in large measure due to the fact that it does not overtax the powers of its teachers and educational leaders, but on the contrary allows them opportunity for the exercise of initiative and encourages a professional attitude towards their work.

6. THE CURRICULUM

The course of instruction in the primary and secondary schools of Norway is uniform for all pupils except in the second and third years of the gymnasium where diverse lines of study are offered. The arrangement is unfortunate in that the individual is sometimes required to pursue subjects of study for which he has no adaptability and in which he can develop no interest. Teachers in Norway tell me that this requirement is a great handicap; retarding the progress of the class, demoralizing the individual, and increasing the burden of the teacher. More flexibility in this regard would doubtless be an advantage. The elective system, so common in our own schools, when rightly supervised preserves sufficient coherence between the studies taken up and gives opportunity for more perfect adjustment.

Not only in the course of study but also in organization, plans of instruction, and equipment, the schools of Norway are too uniform to result in the freest development of the intellect, the richest growth of individuality, or the greatest conservation of time, energy, or money. There are a few variations from their regular routine but these are not sufficiently numerous.

One favorable innovation is the promotion of teachers along with classes through a part or all of the primary school. The consensus of opinion seems to be that better results accrue when a teacher continues with a class through several years of work. This plan is generally followed unless the special fitness of a teacher for work within particular limits renders it highly advisable for assignment to be made to such place. While special aptness for a particular class of instruction should be recognized, the promoting of teachers along with classes generally obviates any tendency to staleness and usually emphasizes special qualifications.

While it would be interesting to discuss the methods used in presenting each subject in the curriculum a few must suffice.

A. Religious Instruction and Moral Education

The church was first to establish schools in Norway, putting them into operation in connection with their cathedrals, probably about the middle of the twelfth century. The chief aim was to prepare the pupils for a religious life, either as ministers or as faithful disciples. Having these as definite ends, the materials for study were selected because of their fitness to contribute along these lines. Instruction was almost wholly in religion. Since morality is such a fundamental part of religion, moral education in large amount was given indirectly. The aim was religion and the result was both morality and religion. Schools came to be generally regarded as institutions wherein moral and religious instruction were the prevailing if not the dominating features. This phase of work early became traditional and gained such momentum that it has ever formed a conspicuous part of every grade of instruction throughout the primary and secondary schools.

During the formative period the instruction in religion maintained a vitality which was quite in keeping with the demands of the times. However, as the school system developed, especially during the closing half of the last century, it became necessary to arrange more definite plans of instruction in religion as well as in other subjects in the school curriculum. The adapting of instruction to the various grades of school work was a difficult task. The adjustment made to needs in the primary schools seems a very happy one. In this elementary section of the school system the instruction in religion consists mainly in story telling. The work is made concrete and personal, and its influence is most excellent.

Not so fortunate has been the attempt to present the great truths and ideals of religion in the secondary grades. The human appeal, so fruitful in the lower classes, does not appear in the higher, at least to the same degree. Instead the work is formal and prescribed. Interest dies out and even respect for the work rapidly wanes as the pupil passes into more advanced grades. I have often thought while observing the listlessness of the pupils during the period for religious teaching that the effects upon morals and religion would be better by far without the instruction as now provided.

To find lodgment in the heart and expression in the experiences of youth, religious principles must be made to appear practical and vital. They must be shown to be desirable in themselves and in their ends.

To teach religion successfully one must be a living example of its true values, an earnest interpreter of its meaning and power, and a sympathetic friend of the pupils. Besides this he must be a genuine teacher with a knowledge of youth and ability to help others obtain a clear conception of the beauty and worth of the nobler life.

Religion and morality are so intimately bound up with life's activities that it is difficult to consider them in and of themselves. It is quite impossible to curriculize and present them as subjects for study and instruction without building up in consciousness the idea that they may or may not be phases of life. When this is attempted it is liable to diminish rather than to increase their true meaning.

It is at least possible that the most favorable results come through specific occasions which arise apart from set requirements. A genuine experience in real life is the best illustration of what morality and religion mean, and it furnishes the most secure foundation for instruction along these lines.

Few lessons and no subjects of instruction can be fully presented without giving considerable attention to their moral and religious phases. If a lesson is completely mastered its moral and religious contributions will have been taken over and appropriated along with any and all other contents. When the moral and religious values inherent in school studies receive their proportionate emphasis there will be no crying need of arranging special courses for their study. The seriousness of the situation at present lies not in the fact that there are no special courses of instruction in morality and religion, but rather in the condition that teachers fail to recognize their opportunities for giving such instruction. They should impress the children with the fact that morality and religion are component parts of life and that they give meaning and reality to every human experience. While it would be gratifying to see these subjects taught as separate branches by individuals who could make them profitable, it is much more imperative that all teachers recognize their own responsibility in this regard, whatever subjects they have to teach.

B. The Classics

In common with those of many other countries, the school curricula of Norway have been saturated with the classics. For a long time the secondary schools were devoted largely to the presentation of the Hebrew, Greek, and Latin languages. About 1850, there arose a demand for an education which was more utilitarian.

Nature study, the sciences, manual training, modern foreign languages, and home economics pressed their claims for recognition and the people became convinced of their values. The masses then began to investigate what right the languages of the ancients had for occupying so large a proportion of attention in school work.

Gradually the ancient classics were replaced by more modern educational materials. Hebrew and Greek were in their turn dropped from the list of required subjects and the time thus saved was given to work regarded as more vital and beneficial. In 1896, a very decisive step was taken when by legislative enactment Latin—the last of the dead languages—was omitted from the list of subjects required in the school curriculum.

This act of the Storthing has been severely criticised by some. However, the people whose right and duty it was to decide studied the matter carefully and thoroughly at home and abroad, and after calm consideration, acted in harmony with their best judgment, passed the law, and put in into immediate execution. The momentum of former practices, the force of tradition, or the example of other nations was not sufficient to control the Norwegian state in its action. It does not permit precedent to determine its policies, foreign nations to do its thinking, nor "well-enough" systems to prevent reform.

When higher ground is seen clearly Norway moves forward with all its power, determined to occupy and utilize the greater opportunities. Such was the condition of the state in its consideration of the classics in their school curriculum. They were willing that those individuals who might elect to pursue the study of the ancient languages should have the privilege to do so and they provided for them such opportunity. However, they were definitely convinced that to require all pupils to study these subjects in order to complete courses of study or enter the university was an injustice. To their credit be it said that when they are convinced that a certain course of procedure is best they have the moral courage to pursue it. In this particular instance the people were fully aware of the fact that they were taking a step which was a decided deviation from the straightforward course pursued for centuries by the leading national educational systems. Yet they became converted to the idea that for their own good, under their own conditions, and looking forward to their future as a state and nation, it would be the wiser solution to leave the classics behind and devote more time and energy to studies which they conceived to be more efficacious.

It is interesting to note the recent tendencies in this direction in other countries. In the United States Latin is becoming less and less a required subject of instruction in the high schools, and each year lengthens the list of colleges which do not require it for entrance. Even conservative and classic-loving Germany has recently opened the doors of her universities to those who have finished the Real-gymnasia. Thus they, too, acknowledge that the way of the classics is not the only road to higher culture and learning.

It has come to be almost universally recognized that the schools exist for the learner rather than the learner for the schools. To debar an individual from privileges for which he is prepared simply because he has not met certain inherited traditional prescriptions is rapidly becoming unorthodox. Norway seems to have set the pace for other nations in at least this one respect, and her clearsighted move in displacing the classics by the introduction of larger amounts of modern foreign languages and other branches of greatest present utility is being followed by other nations of sound pedagogical principles.

C. Physical Culture

Few are the instances where the physical development of the children is so effectually provided for as among the Norwegians. Gymnastics is a regular feature throughout the entire course of study until the completion of the gymnasium. In addition to this the universal rule of requiring the pupils to go into the open air during the intermissions which follow every class meeting has its good effects. Athletic sports also have recently become more important features of school life. Fortunately they have not reached a point of specialization where their values are open to question.

Buildings and grounds are constructed and laid out with the physical welfare of children in mind. As a consequence we find gymnastic halls well equipped and grounds supplied with the advantages most essential in the accomplishment of the desired end, viz., a strong and vigorous body in which to develop a sound mind. Their school grounds are small, making a crowded condition the rule in the larger schools. Strange as it may seem, the same unfortunate condition prevails almost universally in our own land where there appears to be little excuse for congestion. However, the size of the grounds is perhaps a matter of minor importance, especially when compared to their use. Space and equipment may be regarded as incidental; use is the all-important part. Our grounds are not used. We rarely have but one, if any, intermission except the noon hour, the greater portion of which is occupied in going for the midday meal. The results of the Norwegians' enforced, frequent, and regular use of the playgrounds are in evidence on every hand. Robust, vigorous, buoyant, active, healthy, sound, alert, and the like adjectives are the appropriate ones to use in speaking of the physiques of their pupils.

Were the influences of bodily conditions upon mental growth and activity fully appreciated, the schools would doubtless make a sudden shift toward providing adequately for physical education. Physical development has been regarded with considerable favor for some time, but it has usually been a secondary affair when it should have been introduced as a vital feature. Educational systems should provide for the training and development of the physical as well as the mental life. They are dependent upon each other and are in fact two phases of the same life It is obviously wasteful to seek to develop the one without regard to the other, or to attempt the cultivation of one at the expense of the other.

D. Vocal Music

Music is among the most potent factors in developing national spirit and loyalty. Plato wrote: "Any musical innovation is full of danger to the whole state, and ought to be prohibited.... When modes of music change, the fundamental laws of the state always change with them."[44] Napoleon stated that if he might write the nation's songs he cared not who might write its laws. Music in the better forms has moved individuals and nations to great accomplishments, and its efficacy is generally recognized. As a means of education, however, it receives far too little attention.

The quality of music sung in the schools of Norway has some points of superiority. One feature in making it a powerful contributor in developing loyal and competent citizens is the use they make of the best compositions from their own writers. Their poets and musicians have furnished large amounts of excellent productions. They sing of their heroes and of their national ideals and achievements. The spirit in their songs reflects the soul of their fatherland. The influence upon the lives of the pupils contributes to solidarity of the nation and to love for its institutions.

Contrast this with the results of the rattle of rag-time and jigs. Too much of our public school, Sunday school, and church music has been of this order. Public school music and education along this line are matters deserving more attention than they receive. Recent introduction into many schools of victrolas with records of masterpieces produced by the leading artists of the world point to a recognition of the educative value of the better quality of selections. To hear the same productions direct from the soul of the artist would be many times as effectual as any mechanical reproduction, but this is beyond the reach of the masses. Present indications give assurance that the near future will see music more nearly occupying its legitimate place in our educational provisions.

7. LINES OF INSTRUCTION IN THE GYMNASIUM

In the second and third years of gymnasial work three courses of study are open, viz., *Real*, *Language-History*, and *Language-History with Latin*. Here pupils get their first experience in electing the line of work wherein their study shall center. This seems a rather fortunate provision, for by this time likes and dislikes for certain subjects of study, special aptitudes along specific lines, and choice of life work are coming into the foreground of consciousness. The pupils' likes and aptitudes working together influence their decisions concerning life's activities. Again the disposition and nature of individuals render one line of study more attractive and beneficial than either of the others. There are, indeed, many influences at work upon pupils of such age which make it appear highly advisable to follow some particular line of study.

Whether pupils go into the chosen line of life work directly from the gymnasium or by way of the university, it is of distinct advantage to specialize along the line for which they are preparing. Should they intend to teach, they would doubtless prefer studying most the subjects to be taught. In these they would have deepest interest, and from their pursuit they would derive greatest profit. If they determined to study theology, law, medicine, or some other special phase of learning, they would make selection of gymnasial course with that object in view.

[44] Plato, The Republic, p. 424.

Whatever the work to follow completion of the gymnasium, the different courses prepare for the narrower specialization which characterizes life's activities and all their university study.

The following table presents the exact work represented by the three courses in form convenient for comparisons.

TABLE XII.

The Three Courses of Study in the Gymnasia of Norway Showing Weekly Hours Given to Each Subject.[45]

	1			2			3		
	I	II	III	I	II	III	I	II	III
Religion	1	1	1	1	1	1	1	1	1
Norwegian	5	6	6	5	6	7	5	6	6
German	4	3	3	4	3	3	4	3	3
English	4	2	1	4	7	7	4	2	1
French	4	2	2	4	3	5	4	3	3
Latin								7	11
History	3	3	3	3	5	5	3	3	3
Geography		2	1		2			2	
Natural Science	4	5	7	4		2	4		2
Mathematics	5	6	6	5	3		5	3	
Drawing		1	1						
	30	31	31	30	30	30	30	30	30

As the table shows, the three courses are identical during the first year and uniform in religion and German throughout the three years. The Language-History course lends itself favorably for purposes of comparison. It stresses the importance of several modern languages and history, giving to them a preeminence over all other work. The *Real* course reduces the work in English, French, Norwegian, and History and increases the amount of science and mathematics. The course including Latin makes similar reductions but emphasizes Latin instead of the sciences and mathematics.

The Norwegians believe it better and cheaper to offer the different courses in the same school than to provide separate schools. This plan necessitates less duplication and at the same time affords quite as adequate facilities for whatever specialization the different courses represent.

[45] 1. Singing and gymnastics—5 or 6 hours per week are omitted from the table.

2. 1, Real course, 2, Language-History course, 3, Language-History course with Latin.

8. CO-EDUCATION

Whether schools should be co-educational has been a live question among many nations for generations, and considerable time will yet elapse before unanimity of opinion is reached.

Nearly all the schools of Norway are co-educational. However, in some of the city systems boys and girls use different playgrounds, and in certain schools they are segregated also for purposes of instruction. These matters are governed according to the wishes of the inspector or the desires of the principals of the different schools. The aim is to combine the better phases represented in various methods and to adopt the plan best suited to the local situation, or the one to which the person in charge is converted and in which he can, because of his convictions, accomplish best results.

"The separation of the sexes is complete in all the schools of Germany excepting some of the primary classes. The advisability of this is a large question, but by no means a settled one.... Germany feels that she has the proper solution, while in America, with an opposite answer, we feel for the most part satisfied."[46]

In American public schools co-education is almost universally practiced. In reference to this matter we give the opinions of some prominent educators. The lamented Dr. Harris, while engaged in the St. Louis, Mo., schools, wrote: "Discipline has improved continually with the adoption of mixed schools;... the mixing of the male and female departments of a school has always been followed by improvement in discipline, not merely on the part of the boys, but on that of the girls as well. The rudeness and abandon which prevail among boys when separate at once give place to self-restraint in the presence of girls. The prurient sentimentality engendered by educating girls apart from boys... disappears almost entirely in mixed schools."[47] The Honorable John Eaton while Commissioner of Education of the United States made report concerning the co-education of the sexes in several hundred large and small cities in the Union. The tenor of the entire report is well summarized in the following sentence: "We are created male and female; all the impulses and activities of nature enforce co-education; if we must live together we must be educated to that end; to educate separately is an attempt to change the natural order of human economy."[48]

In our higher institutions of learning the situation is much the same. The Commissioner of Education, referring to the State University of Iowa, writes, "The report of the president says that the experience of the institution has uniformly been favorable to the co-education of the sexes; that their influence on each other in the acquisition of learning has been most beneficial as well as conducive to orderly habits. The presence of both sexes is considered 'an invaluable feature' in restraining indecorum and an 'inducement to every virtue.'"[49] The practice has continued with similar results throughout the entire country.

[46] Bolton, F. E., The Secondary School System of Germany, 375.
[47] Report of Bureau of Education, 1891-1892, Vol. II. p. 807.
[48] Special Report, No. 2, 1883.
[49] Report of Commissioner of Education, 1878, p. 71.

Instances favorable to co-education might be multiplied. Its adoption has become a foregone conclusion so far as our general system of education is concerned. True we do have some colleges and a few secondary schools devoting themselves exclusively to the education of one or the other of the sexes. Not many of them are state institutions. They are usually private schools and they answer a certain demand whether well founded or not.

There are certain questions in connection with the education of the sexes which are fundamental and need considerable attention. However, no attempt can be made here to solve the many important problems suggested. It is the intent only to emphasize the necessity of being awake to real conditions and to indicate the fact that herein lies a field for the educator's most careful consideration.

The questions arise: Are the natural functions of man and woman enough alike to justify making their education identical, and will the adoption of such a plan of education result in the advancement or deterioration of the race? A recent article referring "to the endeavor to use women industrially, socially, and politically on the same footing as men" sounds a warning note, crying out against the present tendencies which are taking from the flower of womankind thousands who are eminently fitted for motherhood, "woman's essential function on the globe," and diverting their lives to other and less noble pursuits. "It is therefore essential to the race," say the authors, "that the ablest, healthiest, and finest women should be encouraged, tempted, compelled, if necessary, by circumstances to devote themselves to family life by becoming wives and mothers, and it is doubtful how far it is expedient to draw them off, even for a time to other occupations."[50]

While co-education is in agreement with conditions of family life, is economic, and continues to be entirely practicable, the question still remains whether there may not be justification in a demand for certain fundamental differences to be made in adapting educational means and matter to the two sexes. Co-education, however, may continue without making the education of the sexes identical. In fact it is very easily possible to make the education of the sexes fundamentally different even though both institutions and class activities are co-educational in practice. A difference in the amount of work in certain groups of subjects required of men and women, respectively, might furnish a satisfying solution of this question. And if there are certain branches of study which should belong exclusively to one or the other of the sexes, it is a simple matter to separate for such work. On the whole it seems to the writer highly advisable to educate the sexes together as far as possible.

9. THE SCHOOL YEAR

The regular school year in Norway has forty weeks of six days each. The plan of having school on Saturdays furnishes an additional day of fruitful, well directed activity to the children, who might otherwise be permitted to spend the time in idleness or misguided conduct.

[50] Whetham, W. C. D. and C. D., Decadence and Civilization, The Hibbert Journal, Vol. X. No. 1.

In America we have so many vacations and holidays that our schools are in session only about 75 or 80 per cent of the time utilized in Norway. We may be justified in having the long summer vacations because of the inconvenience and depletion of strength occasioned by the heat, but several of our vacations during the year and the practice of having no school on Saturdays are inheritances without much justification. School activities, when rightly conducted, should be invigorating and exhilarating instead of producing a state of prolonged fatigue requiring seasons of inactivity or other changes in order to regain lost vitality. Again, the relaxation occasioned by diversion of thought and change of activity on Sunday is certainly sufficient to counteract any necessity of using Saturday for recuperation. It appears evident that we are not as frugal in this matter as sound judgment demands that we should be.

10. SCHOOL LUNCHES

It has been found that mental activity is very greatly affected by conditions of nutrition. The quality, quantity, and preparation of foods, together with regularity in eating, determine to a considerable extent what may be the progress of the pupil in his growth, both mental and physical. The child who is improperly fed or underfed is thereby handicapped, while the one who receives intelligent care along the same line is placed at a distinct advantage.

That in all large cities there are hundreds and thousands of underfed children is a fact of common knowledge. In many cities provisions have been made for supplying at least one meal per day free of charge to all needy pupils. Norway has been in the forefront in this paternalistic movement. Several of her cities have undertaken this noble work and probably no city in the world can boast of more adequate facilities for carrying it on than Christiania.

They purchase the best procurable quality of the most nutritious food, prepare it in a wholesome and palatable manner, and send it out from a central kitchen to the several primary schools of the city in such quantities as are needed to liberally supply the demands. The food is served hot in the regular lunch rooms absolutely free to all children whose parents ask it and at first cost to others. This work in Christiania is typical of the provisions made in other cities but the equipment, and possibly the system of distribution, is superior to that found elsewhere.

In addition to this, nutritious and easily digested foods and drinks are provided at other schools and served at a moderate cost in the lunch rooms at stated hours in the day. This latter provision is generally in charge of the family of the janitor of the building and is most common in the private and secondary schools to which the previously mentioned plan does not extend.

Experiment has demonstrated in our own land that it is entirely practicable to provide at a minimum cost warm, well-cooked, wholesome foods to either supplement or replace the cold indigestible lunches so commonly carried by school children. The cities and towns enjoy few if any advantages over the rural districts in this regard. The plan is workable and advisable, and it should be more commonly adopted.

11. COMPARATIVE ATTAINMENTS

In the study of the school system of Norway it is interesting to compare the school life and attainments of the pupils with those of American children. It is true that until we have established norms for measuring the results of education, we cannot make accurate statements regarding the relative standing of pupils nor estimate precisely their accomplishments. However, we are able to single out some features of importance and compare them in a general way.

It has been noted that the Norwegian pupils begin school at seven years of age, while the American children commence at five or six. Many prominent educators believe that our American children start to school too young. They are of the opinion that their development, physical and mental, would be better if they did not begin formal school work until at least seven or eight years of age. The greater physical development of the Norwegians, due to their later start, gives them a distinct advantage. Their bodily strength and vigor supplement and aid their mental growth.

Passing through Norway's successive grades of school to the completion of the gymnasium requires twelve years. The same length of time is used in reaching graduation from our American high school. Now it is generally conceded that a graduate of the gymnasium in Norway is two years in advance of a graduate of the American high school; or in other words a student entering the university from Norway's gymnasial course has an education equivalent to that of an individual entering the junior year of work in an American college or university. Some would rank the Norwegian even higher than I have here suggested; however, only a very general comparison can be made.

In consideration of these conditions the question arises: How shall we account for the fact that we use two extra years in order to reach approximately the same standard? It is recalled that the Norwegian entering school at seven and progressing at the normal rate are ready for university work at nineteen while the Americans begin two years earlier in order to reach the same attainments at the same age. If the Norwegian pupils accomplish as much in twelve years, beginning at seven years of age, as our American children do in fourteen years, commencing at five, should we rest satisfied, or should we modify our system so as to profit by their experience? Why permit traditions or precedent to rob us of choice benefits within our reach?

Again, the students entering the Norwegian university are older and more mature both physically and mentally than are ours. Being older, their habits of life are more definitely formed, and they are better fitted to undertake the responsibility of self-direction. It has been suggested by some that we extend the work of the high school in order to keep our children under parental guidance until they are sufficiently mature to care for themselves at less hazard.

The course pursued by Norwegian pupils is uniform for all until the last two years of the secondary school, when certain branches of study may be chosen for major attention. When students start to the university they enter immediately upon specialized lines of work and pursue them to their limits. The American pupils are privileged to elect a considerable proportion of their secondary school work, yet they do not generally specialize at all until their junior year in college; frequently they postpone definite specialization until the beginning of graduate courses.

Fundamental social characteristics enter into educational ideals, and each nation, very naturally, develops a system of schools peculiarly adapted to its needs. There are, of course, general underlying principles which operate in all educational systems and place them on similar bases; there are also certain features, essential in the make-up of the individual systems, which are not common. These peculiar factors give distinctive character to the various systems and are of telling effect in determining their excellencies. Whether these special phases affect the life and accomplishments of the pupils, the nature of their work, the management of school affairs, or other educational activities; they render the different systems almost impossible of comparison. However, they are suggestive, and frequently they may be modified and used in improving the systems of other countries.

12. METHODS OF INSTRUCTION

Every successful teacher presents his subject in conformity with some universal principles of method. While these cannot be mechanically systematized and used according to unchanging rules, they form a necessary part of an instructor's equipment. The teacher who knows the subject and is master of the technique of instruction is sure of success, while the one without method will fail.

It seems that the pedagogues of Norway have formed a happy combination of some methods of instruction. They appreciate the value of the class meeting and with them "teaching goes on chiefly in what we call the *recitation*. This is the teacher's point of contact with his pupils; here he meets them face to face and mind to mind; here he succeeds or fails in his function of teaching."[51]

The excellence of the work of instruction in Germany has long been recognized. That "the German teacher teaches" is very generally known. He transcends all texts and is an authority on the subjects he presents. By pedagogic training he has been exalted to a place of eminence in his profession. It is possible that they over-emphasize the work of the instructor and neglect the part that pupils should play.

In America various methods of instruction are in use. One plan is to regard teacher and pupils as cooperators in activities wherein interests are common. The teacher, having had experience, exercises control and serves as chief guide through the most critical places in the way of progress. So far as possible the pupils are encouraged to exercise individual initiative and to become independent. They are not to be merely recipients from the teacher's vast store of knowledge, but with him they are to become genuine participators in the world's thoughts and

[51] Betts, G. H., The Recitation, p. 2.

activities.

Another plan in all too common use may be designated as the "text book method." According to it the major portion of information comes from the voluminous, logically developed, well-arranged, and somewhat attractively printed and bound readable text. The function of the teacher is largely testing knowledge gained from books, assigning lessons in the text, supplementing the work of the pupils from his own store or by reference to other works on the subject, and stimulating them to earnest effort in every possible way.

President Hall would not regard this text book plan of work as very worthy procedure. He writes that some teachers take time "telling pupils what to do and testing to see if they have done it. But this is not teaching; but a device of ignorance, laziness, or physical weakness, or all combined. The real teacher teaches and reduces recitation to a minimum. Whoever has visited the best continental schools or studied comparatively such national educational exhibitions as those of St. Louis must have been acutely impressed with the fact that we exhibit what the pupil does, Europe what the teacher does. Here he says, 'Go, do this, and prove to me that you have done it.' There he says, 'Come, let us study together; I know and will inform, interest and inspire you to go on.'"[52]

The instructors in the schools of Norway are true teachers but they do not rely wholly upon their own activity. The text finds a place not so large as in American schools but of some consequence. The pupils are privileged to act on their own initiative to some extent though they are not granted unlimited freedom. They cooperate with the teachers in many lines of school work where they find interest and profit. Demonstration is largely in the hands of the teachers. The testing of lessons studied is a common exercise with them, and their class hours are given to intensive activity in which every individual member is expected to be a participant and contributor. They, like we in America, aim to suit instruction to pupils of average ability rather than to the brightest as they do in Germany and France.

13. CONTINUITY OF EFFORT

By referring to the programs of work arranged for the successive years in the schools of Norway, one readily sees that there is but little variation in subjects of study from the first grades of the primary school to the completion of the gymnasium. The change of greatest importance is the introduction of foreign languages—German and English the first and second years in the middle schools and French the first year in the gymnasium.

When the child enters school he begins subjects of study which represent the several fields of knowledge. The teaching aims to keep him in touch with these in ways adapted to his stage of development. As the pupil grows the scope of each subject enlarges. They advance together. Keeping the subject definitely in mind for a long time tends to the creation of permanent interests and at the same time makes possible its assimilation into the very life of the learner. It becomes vital and usable

[52] Hall, G. Stanley, Educational Problems, Vol. II., p. 295.

after being acted upon in the various stages and conditions of life through which the child passes. Inter-relations and associations with other subjects of study and various phases of life are affected, which give to it distinct values. Too often we find in our own schools that hurried and intensive study of certain subjects does not create permanent interests nor prove of real worth.

If natural forces in the child are recognized and utilized they facilitate the learning process and make school activities profitable and delightful. It is a well attested fact that at certain periods in the psychological development of a child mastery of special phases of learning is easy for him. Courses of study and plans of instruction should be prepared in such a way that the different phases of work included may be presented and stressed while the nascent period of interest is on.

We Americans are given to dividing a subject into its separate phases, studying them consecutively for short periods of time, and then forgetting them. The plan is wasteful and unpedagogic. Note the manner in which we break up the work in mathematics and in the mother tongue. It is questionable whether there be a single valid argument favoring such practice.

The Norwegians present mathematics as a single and comprehensive subject. The same is true in their teaching of the mother tongue. The plan is advantageous from every view point. It is certainly conducive to economy of time and efficient results. Instead of breaking up subjects of instruction and isolating their several phases from each other, we ought rather to keep them intact and set about coordinating the several branches of instruction as closely as possible.

Education should seek to associate and interrelate the truths we obtain and to organize our knowledge into an effectual system. The formation of a comprehensive curriculum, with arrangements for its presentation in harmony with sound psychological and pedagogical principles, is a matter of pressing importance.

While the school systems of the present are evidently superior to what any past generation has known, yet the investigations of psychologists and educationists stress the fact that in many ways they are weak and inefficient. The accumulated experience of the past needs overhauling by masters with insight and foresight. Educational methods and principles which have been tested and proven worthy should be put into operation. Each nation should devise and adopt the most perfect educational system possible, and this then should be carried into execution by an army of qualified teachers responsive to the call for truly consecrated service.

BIBLIOGRAPHY

BOOKS

Erichsen, A. E., *Bergers Kathedralskoles Historie.*

Hertzberg, N., *Paedagogiskens Historie.*

Holst, Axel, *Skolehygiene.*

Monroe, W. S., In Viking Land. Norway: Its People, Its Fjords and Its Fjelds.

Paludan, J., *Det Hoiere Skolevaesen i Danmark, Norge og Sverig.*

Salmonsens Store, *Illustrerede Konversationsleksikon.*

Thieste, J. Schaan, *Byskoleloven med Forklarende Anmerkninger.*

Thieste, J. Schaan, *Landskoleloven med Forklarende Anmerkninger.*

PERIODICALS AND REPORTS

Anderssen, Otto, *Fra Norske Skoleforhold i 1908, Vor Ungdom, 1909.*

Anderssen, Otto, *Fra Norske Skoleforhold i 1909, Vor Ungdom, 1910.*

Anderssen, Otto, *"Norwegisches Schulwesen," Sonderabdruck aus* W. Reins *Encyklopadischem Handbuch der Pädagogik, 2. Auflage.*

Anderssen, Otto, *Skolen for Skolens Opgaver.*

Anderssen, Otto, "The New Laws for the Secondary Schools in Norway," Special Reports on Educational Subjects, Gt. Britain, 8: 168.

Heiberg, J. V., "Education in Norway," Norway (Official Publication for the Paris Exhibition 1900), pp. 266-294.

Nissen, Hartvig, "Public Instruction in Norway," The American Journal of Education, 8: 295-304.

Norsk Skoletidende, Published since 1869.

Pogue, Belle C., "Education and Schools of Norway," Education, 10: 420-424.

Report of the Commissioner of Education of the United States, 1871, 1873, 1878, 1881, 1882-3, 1885-6, 1888-9, 1889-90, 1891-2, 1894-5, 1896-7, 1897-8, 1902, 1903, 1906, 1910.

Skolebladet, Published since 1898.

Thornton, J. S., "Schools Public and Private in the North of Europe," Special

Reports on Educational Subjects, Great Britain, 17: 36-65.

Vold, J. Mourly, Report of Royal Commission of Secondary Education, Great Britain, 5: 640-644.

OFFICIAL PUBLICATIONS

Beretning om Skolevaesenets tilstand i Kongeriget Norge. Yearly since 1861.

Forslag til en forandret Ordning af den høiere Almenskole af den ved kgl. Resolutions af 3 die September 1890 nedsatte Kommission.

Gymnasiet: Lov om høiere Almenskoler; Reglement for de høiere Almenskoler; Undervisningssplan; Eksamensreglement; 1911.

Lov af 9de June 1903 om forandret Prøver ved Universitetet.

Lov om abnørme Børns Undervisning.

Lov om behandling af forsømte Børn.

Lov om det Kongelige Frederiks Universitet.

Lov om Folkeskolen i Kjøbstaederne.

Lov om Folkeskolen paa Landet.

Lov om høiere Almenskoler.

Lov om Laererskoler og Prøver for Laerere og Laererinder i Folkeskolen.

Middelskolen: Lov om høiere Almenskoler; Reglement for de høiere Almenskoler; Undervisningsplan; Eksamensreglement. 1911.

Naermere Bestemmelser angaaende de offentlige Laererskoler og Laererprøver.

Norwege: Lois sur L'Enseignement Public.

Odelsthings Proposition Nr. 36 (1909) om forandringer i Lov om høiere Almenskoler av 27de Juli 1896.

Odelsthing Proposition Nr. 12 (1910): A. Om forandringer i lov om høiere Almenskoler av 27de Juli 1896. B. Om forandring i lov om forberedende prøver ved Universitet av 9de Juni 1903.

Reglement for Aarsprøver, Middelskole-eksamen, og Eksamen Artium. Reglement for de høiere Almenskoler og Undervisningsplan for Middelskolen, 1903.

Reglement for den ved Lov af 18 de Januar 1902 anordnede Optagelsesprøve ved Laererskolerne.

Reglement for det Paedagogiske Seminar og Paedagogisk Eksamen.

Statistisk Aarbok for Kongeriket Norge. Yearly.

Sorthings Proposition Nr. 1, Hovedpost V. (1910) om bevilgning til det høiere Skolevaesen.

Undervisningsplan for Gymnasiet, 1903.

Universitets-og Skole-Annaler. Yearly.

INDEX

A

C

D

E

R

S

T

U

V

W

Printed by Libri Plureos GmbH in Hamburg,
Germany